purplish

THE NEW AMERICAN CANON

The Iowa Series in Contemporary Literature and Culture

Samuel Cohen, series editor

purplish
poetry anger publics

...

José Felipe Alvergue

UNIVERSITY OF IOWA PRESS, IOWA CITY

University of Iowa Press, Iowa City 52242
Copyright © 2025 by José Felipe Alvergue
uipress.uiowa.edu

Printed in the United States of America

Cover design by Anna Jordan
Text design and typesetting by April Leidig

No part of this book may be reproduced or used in any form or by any means without permission in writing from the publisher. All reasonable steps have been taken to contact copyright holders of material used in this book. The publisher would be pleased to make suitable arrangements with any whom it has not been possible to reach.

Printed on acid-free paper

Library of Congress Cataloging-in-Publication Data
Names: Alvergue, José Felipe, author.
Title: purplish: poetry anger publics / by José Felipe Alvergue.
Description: Iowa City: University of Iowa Press, 2025. | Series: New American canon | Includes bibliographical references. |
Identifiers: LCCN 2024044559 (print) | LCCN 2024044560 (ebook) | ISBN 9781685970147 (paperback) | ISBN 9781685970154 (ebook)
Subjects: LCSH: American poetry—Minority authors—History and criticism. | American poetry—21st century—History and criticism. | Anger in literature. | Poetry—Social aspects—United States. | Poetics—Political aspects—United States.
Classification: LCC PS153.M56 A38 2025 (print) | LCC PS153.M56 (ebook) | DDC 810.9/920693—dc23/eng/20241011
LC record available at https://lccn.loc.gov/2024044559
LC ebook record available at https://lccn.loc.gov/2024044560

This book is dedicated to any reader
who cares enough about nation to make your neighbor
a little uncomfortable. To any reader who cares enough about
how future generations will relate to one another
to treat fragility as a temporary condition.

• • •

contents

introduction:
¡chicharros!
1

soma
31

trauma
59

post/nation
87

¡vecinos!
117

dreams
141

notes
167

bibliography
179

index
183

introduction:
¡chicharros!

We used to play a game growing up that went a little like this: someone would punch your arm over and over, and you had to yell ¡chicharros! to make it stop. There was no ceremony to the game. No beginning or initiation. There was no definitive objective that could be called an end. Imagine if you can what this does to one's existence in space. Imagine a game with stochastic rules that expands into space, breaks down predictability and inaugurates some other ethos as the physical rules of a geography. Contextually, the epoch of ¡chicharros! is most aesthetically etched in my mind by a mural visible from the freeway. The 5 as we Californians say. Along an otherwise forgotten wall about twenty feet into a field someone had spray-painted an elaborate and colorful piece with the name of then-governor of California, Pete Wilson, a fiery swastika on either side. This moment in time, the '90s, this location, the Mexico–US border, lives in many people's memories through physical and visual sensations like these. Sensations that filter through our nerves and become perceptions. Imagine the environmental stimuli and the transmissible charge between bodies within the coordinates of a cultural geography, its political history, and what we might call the epidemiological challenge of mitigating stimuli in healthy, adaptive ways. This book braids investigations into national identity via hyperlocal, embodied experiences with the immediate environments individual bodies navigate toward becoming part of a national assembly. I look to poetry, some of it experimental, but all of it by BIPOC and QTPOC artists, to make sense of this movement between individual experience and assembly, and more importantly, the challenges in framing national identity from the emotional physics of coming-into-assembly. Within the contemporary moment of "populist politics" and the expansion of white nationalism in particular, I investigate what it means to live publicly with the responsibility of upholding a civic imagination of futurity through our bodies, all of our bodies, all of our politics, and in the kinds of poetry we make.

Anger is a placeholder.

I grew up on the Mexico–US border in a suburb of San Diego, California, called Nestor. Situated between San Ysidro, America's only "metropolitan" southern border crossing, and the Pacific, knuckled canyons, and urbanization, I experienced the infinitesimal physics and systems of the world in small everyday objects and sensations. Systems that were themselves architectures of toxic principles. The sandy dust that gathered in drifts on the patio tile had traveled entire currents, separated and made fine by the centrifugal spinning of truck tires. The smell of onion fields in the summer wafted into my bedroom before embarking on a vast congested network of containers and consumption. We ran past bats hanging in the stucco entry way of our house, the viral cells inside them living fossils of an ancient watershed that civilizations had relied on for centuries—forgotten little animals of the border whose high frequencies carried the stories of large groups of walkers tracing cyclical trails for clams and acorns and council. Civilizations transformed by swords and disease.

This book is about poetry because as the Salvadoran poet Roque Dalton García said once, "poetry is like bread, for everyone." Poetry is an archive of what we have thought, feared, and loved. What we have desired, longed for, dreamed. Poetry is an archive of somatic and linguistic adaptations to the challenges of living on earth. Poetry is culture. It invokes a human act that can be traced to ochre hand printing, carbon sketches along stone contours inside caves within which our earliest ancestors built flickering fires and imbued their storytelling with moving light, and the warmth that comes from witnessing something temporal. It's also in this lineage that the evolutionary origins of fear have slowly been transformed by governance and politics, deputization, finance, typification and dereferentialization, technologies of all kinds, public events like desegregation, lynching, archives of laws, newspaper clippings, oral history, photographs. American bodies have been transformed by famines and wars, by the pride of property, by the anxiety of ownership. By mobs, fugitive slave patrols, riots, and systemic brutality. Dalton's dream, the diction, is "for," takes a different inflection in this historical imaginary. It precedes the naming of conflict, and the felt pain of some larger logic denying its truth. The denial of this promise lives both historically and, for many, in the neural pathways between broken skin and shattered ideas. Poetry *has not been* for everyone.

Some of us have had to resort to punching each other's arms, to hurting ourselves and others to feel a proxy safety to what language offers by providing our bodies the settled calmness, the stillness that comes from belonging and the sensory reminder of living that comes with touch. Though this book is about poetry, and poetry I say is culture, I focus also on the soma, the body, and track an analytic nuance through somatic health and poetic acts. Immunological signals fire from the sensory organs on our bodies and reach into subperceptible networks of nerves that parasympathetically regulate our sense of safety and anxieties for survival. What we have learned about America is informed by the history of what many bodies have felt during their time as American. When those of us who have been told poetry can only transmit the benevolence of humankind, but, historically, sensory experience triggers a different kinship to social reality through pain, then we have indeed invented poetic form and found our voice to give shape to this paradox.

This is the poetry I'm writing about.

• • •

My curiosity extends from the body into neuroplasticity and wondering how an adaptive awareness might inform a poetics of transformation, and culturally speaking an equally adaptive politics toward the settling of unsettled bodies. I am indebted to the work of Resmaa Menakem on somatic abolitionism, which guides my approach to unpacking poetics, contextualizing politics, referring affect to neurobiological science, and pausing to refocus through my own reflective writing. As he writes:

> Our bodies have a form of knowledge that is different from our cognitive brains. This knowledge is typically experienced as a felt sense of constriction or expansion, pain or ease, energy or numbness. Often this knowledge is stored in our bodies as wordless stories about what is safe and what is dangerous. The body is where we fear, hope, and react; where we constrict and release; and where we reflexively fight, flee, or freeze. If we upend the status quo of white-body supremacy, we must begin with our bodies.[1]

Somatic abolitionism encompasses the processes of this "upending." As a practice this potential belongs to all bodies and is fundamental to the liberation of history as *only* trauma and its rediscovery as temporality, holistically experienced. History, understood purely as trauma introduces potentially unworkable situations of deficit and simultaneously grants authority, though unintentionally, to the very systems of subjection that introduce selective traumatic stimuli. Scientifically speaking, somatic abolitionism encompasses intentional practices that settle trauma responses by focusing on, among other sites, the parasympathetic nervous system. There is a more diffuse benefit, however. Somatic abolitionism involves individual and group therapeutic practices, reflection, writing, breathing, and above all syncing. Through my experiences with somatic abolitionist workshops, I would describe the science behind the group vagal settling as honoring the personal shared space within which worlding takes place in the decisions we carry out while either burdened by stress or liberated from survival instincts constricting our body's ability to freely occupy social bonds. As a writer, recognizing an individual's journey toward remembering ancestral pain parallels what I think lyric and postlyric, and sometimes memoir, can do, which is to reclaim the social life of voice and agency of utterance. This will resonate with poets whose work interacts with historical trauma, American exceptionalism, and ceremonial/ancestral spatial reclaiming. One of the challenges in examining politics and poetry in the presence of the felt is distinguishing personal memory and its power from collectivity. The poets I examine here each practice a kind of experimentalism, which I would describe as postlyric in the sense of a speech act that furnishes the aesthetics of the personal with the adaptive reach of group meaning: the somatic-adaptive matrix of personal history, group stories, and collective possibility. These poets' unique diversities present the opportunity to examine tightly held stories that begin to resemble national experiences once unpacked. This is a group practice, a settling of our trauma response and an abolition of historical injury. We learn that sometimes poetry is political, especially when voice and utterance, memory and corroboration, name the historical systems that mark our bodies. Poetry is most especially political when the vagal-networked minds and bodies gathered around it can witness the social contract as a moment of stolen consent and yet be empowered enough by abolition to untether their futures, treat their traumas, and love themselves.

This to me is an important thread that I wish follow into political contemplation in that the colonial and settler-colonial origins of political reason are also understood by many of us, through our bodies and ancestral stories, to be moments of stolen life, or as Fred Moten posits, "There is a realm and range of modalities of torture whose effectiveness is possible because animated flesh feels."[2] While we may argue that these "modalities" evolve into the microaggressive, to me this only reveals how the sensate flesh of animated bodies has been made strategically visible through their innate nervous expenditure to stimuli, the most dominant of which are felt in and through environments built on stolen consent, and thus illegitimate consensus. My use of somatic abolitionism as a methodology for locating poetics in human practice and against political exceptionalism as the runaway rationale of illegitimate consensus is not just demonstrating a way into experimental BIPOC and QTPOC poetics. Somatic abolitionism is imperative to understanding mind-body/body-mind practices like Menakem's within an ever-evolving, sociohistorical epidemiology. The more empathetically we understanding poetic voice as charged in history, the more significance we might give to public demonstrations of dissatisfaction with the populist status quo, or purple politics, because we must also account for the veracity of a populist environment's effect on a body's lived reality. Or, to express it more directly, a body's neurological activity is historical and immunological. Hormonal survival responses to environmental stress shape our aesthetics, our expressed demonstrations of individual selves cast into communities—especially our responses to those stresses that originate at the rather primitive site of the bond, that body's treatment by others.

I'm making a big assumption about nation: that it could ever resemble kinship in terms of expectations for an ethos of bonding. It's important that I make this point: anger can be a moment of kinship that opens us to a shared experience with vulnerability, and vulnerability is a window facing toward history. Menakem's definition of culture extends from somatic abolitionism toward demystification, principally demystification of how culture functions in America. Culture, via Menakem's acknowledgement of its constituent bodies, requires a decision to engage with something rather painful. And that's because he is a practitioner, not a theorist. Menakem's culture is a plasticity upon which futurial collective health depends, and it asks us to understand how we retain toxic history in active demonstrations of present-day relationships with bodies onto which we project pain—all because we think this path leads to individual survival, and all because we think survival is about an exceptional power over another. Anger, I argue, can be a constitutive force spoken in the unique language of nervous signals. But it's vital to listen, first, to angry voices. There is legitimate somatic knowledge in this kind of anger, though some may find this knowledge distasteful in a "patriotic" sense, in that it first asks to dismantle our education on exceptionalism-as-survival. The fact of survival is very different from beliefs about survival, just as the facts of health differ from the opinions of health first created and sustained through exceptionalism as license for abusive power. My interest is in giving space to somatic-cognitive knowledge pertaining to health as historically constructed and in the shared ritual of deciphering the poetic form of epidemiological circumstances of justice.

The epidemiological paradox is a term that is used throughout public health to describe observable incongruities between US-born and non-US-born members of a shared ethnic or racial group. The immigrant paradox, for instance, studies the positive health markers between latine communities. Some studies compare immigrant children to their US-born peers; other studies compare groups of middle-aged men. There are many other examples, including paradoxes in gestational health, diabetes, anxiety, and depression, as well as more socially stigmatizing diseases like addiction. What do we do with the correlational story of these paradoxes? José Estaban Muñoz applies the idea of an epidemiological paradox in theorizing "Brown" futurity, noting the paradox inherent to bodies that perform survival in the face of environmental stimuli organized around necropolitical desires.[3] Muñoz's project of unpacking Brownness, indeed an extension of his most notable work in *Disidentifications*, was cut short by his death. He was looking for a way into identity that does not rely on the theoretical foundations of identification. Those are sullied pathways scripted coevally with exceptionalist criteria for social freedom and selective political rights. Epidemiology unsettles static frameworks for thinking about subjectivity and identity and begins to include correlational variables, environment, and heritability, even if incompletely. Together, the nervous system, the soma as epidemiologically and immunologically contingent, and cognitive function begin to flesh out that which can be called "the body," or embodiment. But we don't yet see the full picture of affective demonstration and survival, environment and futurity, not entirely as a method for poetic sensemaking.

Learning about emotions, specifically how your body creates them like some kind of phenomenal power to rift one's surrounding ambience, you simultaneously learn about belonging. I belong and have belonged, culturally speaking, to a historical environment that requires membership to pain as a temperature, an atmosphere even. The lessons imparted are that of desensitization to the injury of simultaneously acknowledging that, culturally speaking, your body is assigned a negatively felt value that decreases your social stock. What you learn from political history is that American exceptionalism makes this kind of classification permissible. And exceptionalism is an attractive social system designed to mimic adaptive, or evolutionary belonging. Through this systemic disavowal of emotional truths, a disillusioning silence defines the alienating experience of feeling something publicly. But we've had modes of address at our fingertips also, disqualified ones, impermissible ones. Exposure to the chronic stress of cyclical pain and disqualified feelings has significant lasting effects on the recipient body and their nervous system, on the bystander and their moral imaginary, as well as on the administrator of pain and their self-conceptualizing world views on power, domination, property, and politics. There's no denying it.

Genre, according to Travis M. Foster, becomes in America a rhythm. Genre encompasses processes through which the "reproduction and affirmation" of value embraces a textual turn toward print forms of "address" that facilitate the popularization of dominant, aestheticized beliefs into institutions of the everyday.

> This process occurs in part through the very form that genre assumes: a regularized recurrence, a rhythm. Put differently, genre comes into being through the regularized repetition of its iterations, each of which amounts to a temporal beat that echoes the past and creates anticipation for the future. A meeting ground for memory and expectancy, genre makes and fulfills promises.[4]

My focus on the nervous system, my nervous system, and on the sense of a nervous system through poetic demonstrations of negative affect is a way into thinking about these "collective promises" in America across a time dilation, though located in the zenith of dysfunction in this last decade. The nervous system, moreover, as a biological demonstration of prediction-making has me thinking about memory in a cultural tension. The nervous system as we understand it is a correlational demonstration of two separate activities of the soma, the sympathetic and the parasympathetic nervous systems: what I expand upon later as the vagal network. The somatic-cognitive connection I draw travels through these nervous systems. Its availability exists sensibly, which is where I understand poetry to exist. Specifically, this somatic-cognitive approach makes me wonder how poetry as a genre, as a social form of language that "makes and fulfills promises," also demonstrates what Jonathan Culler calls a "vatic" address.[5] A vatic address is a predicting utterance. This is not merely prophetic as a performance of time: the vatic assembles futurity via the physics of event coming into cognition. The significance for this lies in how neurobiologists understand the predictive operations of the brain and its networked reliance on exteroceptive information to map an environment in adaptive ways.[6] Coming into a correlational experience sensed through both intentional and autonomous nervous response, we, now addressing bodies and not just a particular group, feel something about the predictive connections that either strengthen our survival or put our survival at risk. When stimuli overwhelmingly put some bodies' health at risk, the anger those bodies disclose speaks an important truth about the social context through which selective well-being is permitted to operate in categorical ways, whether racialized, gendered, ableist, or classist. This anger is distinct from "grieving" the status quo, particularly in terms of the loss or potential loss of a supremacist social normativity, or what is called American exceptionalism.

Dilation best describes being able to move between body and context, history and environment. This term can also be used to outline my methodology as an organic attention to more than one discipline at a time. Rather than ration out my attention span in measures of analysis or citational performativity, my attention dilates like a lens. Dilation is very close to impossible, textually, because the result is more like radial bursts (not plateaus) of analysis. As I've gotten more accustomed to myself, I can say that my problem is with representationalism. The connection I sense between my critiques of certain political frameworks and aesthetic frameworks can be reduced to a differentiation between representational assumptions about the event aesthetics brings toward the senses, as well as the correlational sensemaking that takes place in the immediate experience of the event itself. Dilation, moreover, encompasses the historicity of my engagement. One that cites the settler-colonial origins in current-day white-body supremacy and seeks to demonstrate how the exceptionalism inherent in the populist fantasy of a "purple" political identity—as the culmination of a democratic moral identity in the red-blue stalemate unearthed in America's Heartland following Trump's first presidential campaign—affects bodies through the banalization, and spectacularization of intentional traumas.

White-body supremacy, terminology I take from Menakem, exists in a mycological network of reverberating narratives that have historically legitimated abuse through empowering "white-bodies" to write and rewrite the legal modes of governance that ensure the safety of whiteness itself across all realms and scopes of life. I put "white-bodies" in quotes because it's important to understand that even white folks exist in the shadow of this standard, an exacting mythology of power and purity that has operated throughout the Americas. The standard is one of agency, political ability, wealth, and elective identity under god. It has relied on religio-secular rubrics to measure the exactitude of sociocultural demonstrations of identity-supremacy, which is why throughout this book I use the denominations of white Christian nationalism, white nationalism, and white supremacy somewhat interchangeably. The networking of morality, law, force, and performativity have worked in concert to sanction violence: lynching,[7] enslavement, rape. The history of white-body supremacy lives inside institutions we rely on today for ensuring modes of governance: the carceral archipelago, the judicial and criminal justice system, electoral mapping, housing, education, and more. As a standard against which citizenship has historically been legitimated, white-body supremacy includes the narratives regarding mental and emotional health as a public concern. White-body supremacy is also, I argue, a foundational evil to the logic of beneficence upon which the American body politic has been philosophically defined.[8] Never mind the story we are told, like children sitting in the lap of our granite parent.

• • •

When poets reconstruct a possible world of the felt, where do we, collectively, archive the intentionality of negativity as a response to correlational information about the social paradoxes of a political sphere interested in justice but inside of which permissible injustice continues to threaten the health of many? This book is about the cognitive-somatic reality of existing right now, examined through poetry and politics and thus sensed through various transparent

introduction

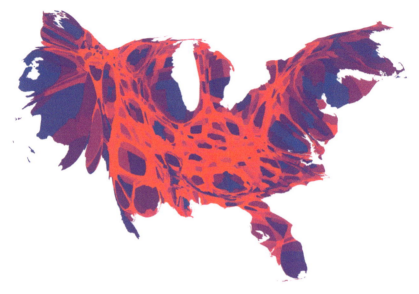

FIGURE 1. Election cartogram, Mark Newman © 2016.
https://creativecommons.org/licenses/by-sa/3.0/deed.en.

and veiled archives organizing experiential evidence of correlational feelings regarding aesthetic and political history in North America. Purplish reality, though it encompasses the "now," cannot be understood without attending to a cascade of somatic-cognitive adaptations from previous manifestations of spectacularized exceptionalism masquerading as nationalism and hiding in aesthetic truth.

To understand this, it's important to disentangle representational promises from the correlational story of where we are.

Mathematicians and cartographers like Robert Vanderbei and Mark Newman have been experimenting with electoral maps with alternative standard representational systems for visualizing results precisely by not relying on a static understanding of spatial experience. Newman's cartograms, for instance, use a collective sense of space and territory, the "map" of the United States, to demonstrate correlational spatial experience through political affiliation.[9]

I use the term correlational here in place of representation to draw attention to an agnosticism over form, binarism, and operation. Important to my project is the writing itself, my writing. I want to start introducing a productive collaboration between a poetics of feeling and a political science of experience because the cultural moment of purple politics reflects a troubling confluence of permissible and impermissible public feelings. One can trace this conflict to Reconstruction, perhaps even earlier to political Modernity and the erection of public spaces as realms organized around the treatment of ungodly bodies. It's not just been my experiences in the Midwest that underscore how white nationalism is reestablishing a cultural supremacy by coopting publics and policing political agonism by unraveling, in seemingly polite ways, the public safety of BIPOC and QTPOC bodies. "The electoral earthquake of Donald Trump's presidential campaign and victory," notes the geographer Adam Jadhav in their ethnographic study of contemporary rural populism, "thrust mostly white, mostly conservative rural geographies—especially the Midwest—into a political spotlight."[10] Brought into the spectacle of focus, and normalized by its banal visibility, "[p]olarized, popular discourse frequently presents this rural political imaginary as a bastion of regressive and insular politics, juxtaposed with supposed liberal, metropolitan pluralism." Rural populism has come to stand for a cultural permissibility of expansive white Christian nationalism and white-body supremacy, and justifies itself through claims to romanticized principles of American exceptionalism: "the long death spiral of American manufacturing; envy and resentment at being 'left behind' by burgeoning, urban, creative classes; open racism, misogyny, religious bigotry and/or heteronormativity raging against perceived threats; overdetermined hatred of Hillary Clinton; and a Democratic Party that presumes superiority over the 'country bumpkin.'"

Purple populism as a euphemism for white Christian nationalism also nuances public demonstrations of negativity between the realized anger of those threatened by sanctioned injustice and those who have been encouraged to mobilize grievances with progressivism or expansive rights. Loss, in other words, especially loss experienced through the dismantling of exceptionalism, is not the same thing as anger here defined. With this ethnographic picture in mind, and returning to visual representations of rural populism, purplish manifestations reveal a correlational trauma, a violence, a bruising of sorts where exceptionalism punches away at veneers of civility, punches away at the healthy tissue of communities and neighborhoods. The richest purples are the most pained sites of this game.

"Politics" correlates with the most "lyric" moments in my life, moments

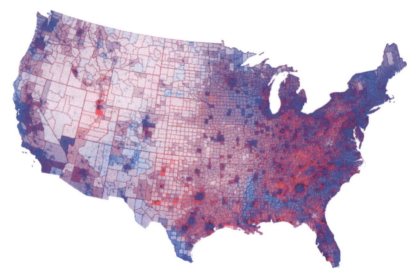

FIGURE 2. *What America Looks Like*, Chris Howard © 2012.
https://creativecommons.org/licenses/by-sa/3.0/deed.en.

coded into my intellect and disposition by factors of love, fear, and confusion. Factors of spatiotemporal dilation, the expansion and contraction of stimuli as forms of violence or care, interact with my body in a continuity institutionalized as practices theorized into justice. Justice is not representational. It should not be, though its becoming national has relied on precisely the aesthetic dimension of representational exceptionalism. Justice, I argue, is correlational. That doesn't bridge the gap, however, between my lyric and archival political consciousness. Lyric experiments into utterance do, on the other hand, animate a correlational matrix, and this is what I seek to explore.

A missing piece to this full picture is who I am and why that matters. Why it matters that I am an immigrant, and that I lived through the xenophobic, authoritarianism of southern California's border wars during the '80s and '90s—an atmosphere so thick with fearful somatic stimuli that ¡chicharros! seemed nothing more than wallpaper inside the dwelling of our exemption from Americaneity. It matters that I decidedly turned to poetry, so-called experimental poetry in particular, in a romantic attempt to name my anger without relying on representational ready-mades. Southern California's xenophobia was made permissible through representational justice, and it interlocked like a double helix to specters of political Modernity and the Eurocentric pseudoscience that exploited phenotypification to define moral personalities and the reciprocal political potential moral personalities represent. One of the most detrimental personalities to collective identificatory health, I argue, is the performative "goodness" that arises in an environmental assumption of "mutual fairness."[11] I interrogate John Rawls and this idea of the good because I have experienced the cultural exceptionalism of its fundamental assumption of "fairness" undergirding justice to be the most fungible rationale across demonstrations of white-nationalism-as-normative publics. Goodness and fairness are the cornerstones of purplish populism. Its politeness grants spatial permission to racial nationalism and religio-secular authority. According to Rawls, "mutuality," being already "implicit in the principles of justice," permits political personalities to adhere to "justice as fairness" through "an appreciation of what they do as an element in our own good."[12]

As Jacques Lezra so aptly puts it, however, "It would be nice, so nice . . . having a single world in common . . . having similarity and subjectivity."[13] My approach to politics, as a poet, is via the methodological necessity to unsettle the consensual epoch from which theory gathers representationalism. There is no consensual epoch in traditional political thought, no time whatsoever where consent is a universal assumption. The consent/consensual assumption is pure exception. It crafts the determinism from which populism gathers its social authority over "other" bodies.

There is another dimension to this critique, which again opens up to the methodology of this book being agnostic to linearity—of thought and time—which I would describe through Matthew Scully's lens of aesthetics and political repudiation, "dissensual anachronism."[14] The spatiotemporal arrangement of dissensus, action, and anachronism provides sensible access to the "*longue durée* of democracy in the United States without reinscribing a consensual narrative, and it also enables focus on . . . equality across these spatio-temporal configurations." Scully argues for a framework that "follows the achronological and errant drive of democratic equality." My framework locates such a drive in the adaptive responses of the lived somatic-cognitive realities of the subjectivized in America, whose very attention to bonding and soothing through often conflictual possibilities reassembles collectively embodied expressions of survival and the human assumption that we exist toward a future shared between generations.

I live in the Midwest now. I raise my kids in the toxicity of what is often called a purple political atmosphere where red and blue party dispositions swish and swirl to create a new identity. At least that is the romanticized portrayal of what a purple political identity represents. But my lived experience is less than romantic, and my body tells me that living purplish is less about politeness toward ideological variation and subcultural idiosyncrasy than it is about beating through the very health of political agonism and making sure that the dominant settler-colonial moral personality remains at the representational center of our collective political imagination: at the representational center of nation itself.

When purple electoral maps first started appearing on social media and in news outlets, regional epicenters of electoral tension, or swing districts, primarily in the Midwest, quickly latched on to narratives of normalcy in the mixture of different ideological cultures. The idea that purple most realistically represents normal political personalities belies an insidiousness: namely, that any faction of white-body supremacy, as a directive on how to justifiably dehumanize unlawful bodies, is normal. As the software engineer and illustrator Chris Howard also points out in his purple election map (figure 2), however, the hueification of red and blue into purple reveals another disturbing reality about our politicization of electoral voice; that is, the traditional coloration of electoral maps correlates to an imbalance between population density and electoral representation. Binarism, in other words, is not statistically a normative status quo in the sense of population. "Such a map performs visual tricks," Jahdav notes. "First, even if politics could be reduced to a binary choice for the individual voter at the ballot box, the politics of a people at geographic scale cannot. In the map's own color schema, all jurisdictions might be better understood as only shades of purple." "The map," he concludes, "confuses a measure of space with a measure of concentration."[15] What happens, socially, in the purple, however, is not pleasant.

Representational imbalance tells another story, which is the story I'm interested in retelling. This story can be explained through, one, the historic "Blue Wall" that electoral politics in the Midwest had, up to Trump's presidency, relied upon for a structural rationality to explain political binarism; and two, the breaking down of that wall by the far right by relying on seemingly cultural moral-historical principles that reinstated somatic-cognitive desires for belonging and acceptance in white-body society. This desire, moreover, is historical, and I trace it back through time to Reconstruction, during which white northerners decided sympathy for newly disenfranchised white southerners was more moralistically important than protecting the newly acquired civil rights of their Black neighbors. Ida B. Wells for instance situates the propensity and permissibility of lynching throughout America precisely in a corroborative white-body supremacy. She indicts this sort of purple post–Civil War identity through its "sanction" of murder under polite consideration for the mythos of a white feminine virtue in need of state-sanctioned protection.[16] In this moment and in that moment, this purplish world, what did it feel like to live in a body charged with a spectacularized invitation for sanctioned violence? This book is about how my body and how other bodies targeted by the xenophobic expansion of justice and the eugenic cleansing of morality have felt, how what we have felt and continue to feel is part of an underappreciated mnemonic nationalism in America, and it looks into these feelings to turn a game of violence into strategies of care.

• • •

When we played ¡chicharros! we were just passing the time. We were filling the time with haptic joy. But we were doing something else too. We were addressing violence. Maladaptively for sure. But the maladaptation was a necessity within a public network that never meant to create spaces for collective or communal health, at least not for us. Which is not to say exceptionalism has been ignorant of expenditure or embodiment, per se. Because it has not. Quite the opposite in fact. Its hyperfocus on bodies has been, always, at the foundation of its logistical mindset. Exceptionalism's raison d'être is the transformation of the body's haptic openness into an expenditure machine, and such a transformation, a nonconsensual one, implicates the entirety of social contracting, in that no such agreement exists in a pure state of fairness but rather only as extensions of exploitation. Our hapticality was a public network between the border and the assumed untraversability of the Pacific, the segregation of the city itself partitioned by freeways, the whole of us a giant amorphous waffle of logistics and neighborhoods, zoning laws and assumptions. Our hapticality existed historically to instill in young bodies that the labor they should occupy themselves with should only be servile, physical, capitalized, and neoliberal. Any other application of our expenditure, which is a haptic potential, a feel, was treated as fugitive. And so I think fondly of

FIGURE 3. Purplish neighbors politely calling me an illegal immigrant, Eau Claire, Wisconsin, 2020.

¡chicharros! also. In fact, as I was writing this book I was reminded about ¡chicharros! by my brother, who lives far away from me, and my first instinct was to remember his body close to mine. Hapticality in this context of fugitivity is a reorientation of sorts, one explained best by Harney and Moten in their now often cited work, *The Undercommons*.

> Hapticality, the touch of the undercommons, the interiority of sentiment, the feel that what is to come is here. Hapticality, the capacity to feel through others, for others to feel through you, for you to feel them feeling you, this feel of the shipped is not regulated, at least not successfully, by the state, a religion, a people, an empire, a piece of land, a totem. Or perhaps we could say these are now recomposed in the wake of the shipped. To feel others is unmediated, immediately social, amongst us, our thing, and even when we recompose religion, it comes from us, and even when we recompose race, we do it as race women and men. . . . Though forced to touch and be touched, to sense and be sensed in that space of no space, though refused sentiment, history and home, we feel (for) each other.[17]

To figure out what's going on with you, why you do the things you do, feel the way you feel, takes work. It takes time, it is collaborative, it is laborious. We were told from an early age that the only work we were meant for belonged to some other power that we'd never be a part of. Not fully recognizing the ability to network our nervous unsettlement by coopting the haptics of our interrelatedness and political identity within a historical continuum, we turned to what was there. I think having the clarity of Harney and Moten's recounting of dissensualism would have saved us. Poetry of anger is poetry in dissensuality; it is haptic, a poetry of vulnerability. Many of us, a community that extends beyond the poets and artists I study in this book, are exploring these histories, personal and shared, in front of an audience that may or may not know what we're thinking through. Many also feel it and feel us feeling through them feeling. We take a risk in our poetics, unsure even about how our families will respond. And it's scary. It's scary also for me to think that I'm a state employee, and my office location is public information. Fugitivity is still at the end of the day fugitivity. My course syllabi could easily show up in some far-right chatroom used to radicalize young men through the misappropriation of republican principles or Christianity. I've been interrogated by campus police at two different institutions. For those of us in the South or the Midwest, it's downright dangerous in light of attacks on CRT and the use of social media to fan the flames in lone wolves. For the poets who are also trans, undocumented, queer in any way that American readers decide is transgressive, the fear of harm is real. And so when I talk about hapticality and feeling, that is as real as the reality of harm.

¡Chicharros! was a stand-in for the stochastic. Contained pain was a stand-in for dominance: for agency, in fact, but this would have to be unearthed years later. Walter Mignolo argues that what is sentient in decolonial aesthetics is a "sensibility" that liberates *aesthetis* from the "aesthetic." *Aesthesis* refers to the sensorial network of the work that creates opportunities of stimulation, and thus functions within the work as the spatiotemporal rift through which the audience observes "reexistence," *re-existencia*. Not "resistance," Mignolo clarifies, but a reexistence that creates subjects "disobedient" to the colonial imperatives hiding in the aesthetics of the epoch within which existence has been coopted by colonialism.[18] In the absence of true sentience, agency can only be found in the transparent, and violence is perhaps the most explicitly transparent personality trait we, back in the '90s, could find. What we searched for was reexistence through it, and through the anger that like an aura surrounded us. It's how we found ways to be accepted. When I think of my most deplorable neighbors, now, and their behavior during Trump's rise to power, I ask, are they guilty, at a fundamental level of somatic truth, of anything more than wanting to belong or be accepted? I'm curious to know, being so close to it, what their version of ¡chicharros! is, since theirs are white bodies gifted public sanction to punch Others, instead of themselves.

Poetry, in its disinterest in certain forms of power, coalesces through performance without having to rely on other symbolic frameworks like exceptionalism or capital to do so. With poetry underneath it, the assembly itself enters an alternative demonstration of bodies-that-have-come-together. The performative nature of poetry's reality, the social existence of poetic texts, is part dilation and part framework for readdressing the political limitations on the vatic assembly-coming-to-be nation, community, neighborhood, region, and so on. The poet's present stretches from the speaker's emotional memory, located in a historical goo that has been spread across lands and water by bodies in motion.

An attention in motion is the aspirational horizon of what I wish to accomplish, a brief vision of an assembly without value, agnostic to "promises" and responding only to the challenge of adapting, together, through the sobering and enlightening knowledge of memory and toward the shared expectation of survival. At present, purplish identity in America keeps us from risking the necessary departure from "value." The partnership of whiteness and power under capital casts a bright spotlight on the felt valance of what psychologists call "social learning," and normalized white-body supremacy provides too rewarding a promise of felt acceptance to be passed up by those who misunderstand culture to be merely a fraternity of operationalized dominance.

Playing ¡chicharros! normalized what we experienced as randomness, though knew deep down that we were in the presence of injustice. It projected a framework that guided us through relation, as a system of time—as a chaotic and spontaneous organization of violence—so we could belong to ourselves while experiencing dissociative traumas. I think back now and wonder if we were engaging in a maladaptive therapeutic act. A sort of proto-ketamine treatment for the sustained exposure to denigrative language and for the national narratives about young people of color that dominated the formative decades of my youth, which I understand now as being in a continuum with precedent rhetoric and contemporary permissible dehumanization. We could laugh and endure pain in a simultaneous space-time. We forgave the violator, who was not a violator but a trusted friend. We lived with bruises, all of us, like tattoos. I think back to our environment and am often angry at how adults failed us. How many of them passed down dysfunction and permitted true historical violence, structural violence, to encompass our experiences with publics.

"Culture," Menakem explains,

> creates a sense of belonging.... More than anything... belonging makes our bodies feel safe. This is why culture matters to us so deeply.
>
> We humans want to belong. We experience belonging—or the lack of it—in our bodies. We experience it deeply. When we belong, we feel that our life has some value and meaning.[19]

We want this so bad, to belong. We want it so much that we are willing to substitute "likeness" or "acceptance" for true belonging as the contentment of being validated as oneself, encouraged to name oneself, without censoring the emotional histories of positive self-making. "Culture is how our bodies retain and reenact history," writes Menakem. Scientists Peter Richerson and Robert Boyd distinguish between "social learning" and "culture" by clarifying how large scale "learning" through imitation does not in actuality create adaptation.[20] Imitated behaviors replicate in a cognitive context of "belonging," by way of appearing similar. This behavior exhibits the physics of what I am calling exceptionalism. So while a population might "retain" and "reenact," as Menakem points out, that group is not coalescing into a culture premised on adaptive evolutionary gains through a predictive consciousness or somatic-cognitive awareness. The culture that adheres to the technical requirements of exceptionalism remains stagnant in its enforced homogeneity. This enforcement replaces survival as a poetics shaped by memory's aestheticization of survival. "Culture," Richerson and Boyd argue, "is highly adaptive" allowing "populations to accumulate complex . . . tools and institutions." The kind of anger that pours like an anthem for groups, for cultural tribes, tells us something about the history we have lived with for the last few decades. It tells us something about how we have adapted through dissociating empathy. Our innate capacity to care has been weaponized, and what we are taught to think of as a collective practice has been disclosed to us through interactions with culture as a capacity to inflict pain as a reflexive instinct to define what is personal by securing tribal safety, even a fantasy of safety from equally fantastic monsters and threats. In fact, it may be uniquely a "safety" from this colonial imagination of the Other. What about "our" safety from racial supremacy, its violence, its viral epistemological monopoly?

"Safety" in America is a loaded term. I live in Wisconsin, and I am bombarded with ads in my social media for tactical pants that allow wearers to conceal handguns and knives. These are pants designed for the modern warfare American men are taught they must fight out in neighborhoods and parking lots, school board meetings, and soccer fields, all in defense of their way of life and for the safety of their families and property. The story goes that for the entire trip from El Salvador to America my mother never let go of my body. I think about her holding me every time one of my kids asks to be picked up or to ride on my shoulders, realizing that our earliest sense of safety is most strongly felt at times of perceived vulnerability. Glimpses of fatigue press our sense of possibility up to a precipice, and we must make an embodied decision.

How do I articulate this anxiety at the somatic level of adrenaline that I am also told is asocial? How do competing narratives of vulnerability challenge the violent, yet normative sense of threat Americans attempt to quell with guns or force? How do I connect with my neighbors who have no somatic foundation for feeling what I feel as a manner of being American?

I'm talking about a civic imaginary when I refer to publics in this way, to the bonds facilitated in *aesthesis* and rooted in the haptic re/making of worlds from the ontological ruins uncovered by critical learning. As such I'm referring to the historical reality of publics in America as a concept of social responsibility following the Civil War and Emancipation, on the one hand, and on the other, in an even further historical sense, the transformation of public life during hemispheric colonialism, and the definition of qualified and disqualified bodies based on casta. Here I mean casta as an aesthetic system that extends beyond paintings, as it is most often engaged with today, that is, as a logic extending into law, family systems, financial typification and derivation, and beyond. In our American context of civic reexistence, it's understood that Emancipation unsettled the term "civic" in populist discourse, and as George Washington Cable points out, white southerners purposefully replaced "civic" with "social" when debating the new responsibilities of equal citizenship.[21] As he argues, the white southerner feared the chaos resulting from public relationships with Black persons who just moments before had been considered private property. The fear of this "chaos," where civil bonds were to replace legal bondage, reveals the nature of order in America. The poet Albery Whitman, whose epic poem *The Rape of Florida* I examine, further states in an often-quoted address to the Black community titled "The Bugle Note" how white comradery after the Civil War reshaped racial supremacy through the vote, through the economy, and through reifying, socially influential narratives around political principles by bridging class and regional differences among white people in America. A twentieth-century white-body exception was born out of the shattered remnants of divided families and racial panic affecting white people after Emancipation. The white northerner's sympathy for the unsettled and disappointed white southerner was a far greater negative than any guilt they might have felt for centuries of being complicit in enslavement and murder.

Thus, it's important to note that while Menakem centers the body as the vessel for feeling pained, the physics of the injury that pains, that brings pain, is neurological. The body demonstrates and processes signals that accord meanings to the images, sensations, and predictions that form the nebulous universe often simply called "memory." Whitman's bugle call, and indeed his poetry, as does the work of the other poets I read here, reestablishes a connection to the affective swell "we" feel as members of social groupings complexly influential on history, influenced as we are, each of us, by memory. While sociality is fundamentally psychological, our psychology is inherently plastic and adaptive. There is no value, as such, especially any cultural value, to form, implicitly. Such is Catherine Malabou's claim on "plasticity" as well. The natural agnosticism of form reveals to us why it is important to recast "culture" as an organic assembly at the center of adaptive matrices, change, and even evolution.

I think if we're going to interrogate culture, however, we should include its artifacts, including its literatures. We should include those things that have become aesthetic in place of true *aesthesis*. Our individual bond to a lyric arc, the arc of survival through adaptation, intersects with personal histories through which we, as individuals, learn about emotion as an expressive demonstration within intimate emotional units. We are constantly learning, adapting bodies. This operation can easily self-select, can effectively be exploited when under the influence of a societal pressure that mimics adaptation through eugenic assumptions about value, which are in reality nothing more than colonial tactics to erase people's innate method of belonging to history. I hope to parse this further as I move through the poetry.

• • •

What is the form of justice? Assuming it is such a thing as has form. We know, we feel when we are in the presence of justice. Equally we know when we have witnessed injustice. We pass this feeling along more regularly maybe, being able to describe its every contour and detail. The poetry I am talking about is exploratory. It travels between realms of civic reason and apparitions. It goes fully into that space by leaving the civic stasis behind and venturing into the upside down. A poetics of anger comes back to the text, to the performance of speech with knowledge from those worlds. But it's a changed knowledge, a knowledge that embraces uncertainty as merely a ghost that has yet to appear. How many times can a ghost pop its spectral face in front of yours before you can whisper, *chicharros*?

My expertise as a scholar is admittedly not scientific or political, but rather on poetic movement. And by this I don't mean discreet poetic generations or schools, but poetry as a temporal form of arrangement toward the expression of sensations. Movement. This is why a lot of my work seems personal. As sensations flow through my body there are shadows bridging the transparency of ideas with the edges of experience. That's my experimentation. I don't intend hyperbole to mask a gap here. In fact, I would argue it's important to remember what poetic language is, beyond the marketplace of poetic texts or a poet's social popularity. It is, I argue, a record of emotional evolution. This term, evolution, moreover, comes down to adaptations patterned through embodied responses to stimuli. For me, to me, the political sphere has existed as an exhibition of intentional stimuli, and the poetry I think alongside arranges politics and its environment through expressions of feeling that most intelligently unveil what purple politics means to accomplish in its alignment with American exceptionalism.

To accomplish this in *purplish*, I fugue between poetic analysis and personal memory. I delve into reviews of scientific literature and place it all in conversation with political ideas. Aside from Albery Whitman, all the poets I include here are contemporary. Their bodies matter, and it is made apparent in their work that embodiment and history are not truths language can sidestep. Their bodies cannot be represented, they are not representational. This requires a unique way of reading. The insistence of an identity, though one that disobeys identity, is often gathered under the umbrella of postlyric. To me what matters is the lyric continuity and attending to an *aesthesis* of voice.

In my career, up to this point, I've had to investigate what it is a poet does and what it is a scholar does. The *aesthesis* of voice and the historicity of public identity as a context for the sort of citizenship verified in everyday worldmaking is a good place to start. A commonalty these poets seem to share is that the two imagined identities can be thought to participate in the ceremony of beginnings. Ceremonies carry with them a glimpse of a risk, in that ritualism necessitates a departure. As such I recognize the danger of "uncanniness" in what I am doing, in that what I've repeatedly called dilation initiates rituals at each of its boundaries of awareness and introspection. Each time the ritual is a beginning, but not without resonance, and I purposefully elide foundation in the form of an intellectual school or era of criticism. Doing so risks a "catalogue of infinite cases," to use Edward Said's caution against uncanny beginnings upon beginnings.[22] My writing style embraces the potential risk of "being embarrassed" by the beginnings of awareness, and the critical transparencies disclosed in the social contexts of our politics and in the aesthetic assumptions of some semblance of an assembly we might call culture, as well as what may be revealed in mapping the "continuity" of cultural history between these two coordinates within which human feeling can be placed. But this risk is far less risky than letting a moment pass to preserve the decorum of operational thinking and academic register. In short, I think Said's concern with the "career" of a writer, and I would assume with the institutions from which mine garners legitimacy, does not have a place in my thinking. In fact, I would argue that enough has transpired between Said's original project and recent critiques and reoccupations of the University to unsettle that concern, giving us more time and energy to focus on what matters in our thinking: our health.

The soma is without a school of criticism, really, though affect studies, performance studies, and the broader health and humanities are currently addressing embodiment in fascinating and liberatory ways. I address the soma as a parasympathetic and simultaneously socialized assembly in the next and last chapters, "soma," and "dreams." "Soma" unpacks the role of nourishment and vagal soothing in the work of Dorothy Chan, Joshua Nguyen, and Elizabeth Alexander as a way of defining modes of bonding possible when bodies attend to parasympathetic needs and desires, while in "dreams" I look to Divya Victor and Claudia Rankine and what I call their gestational poetics as a way of framing the question of epigenetics in transgenerational trauma. Because the epigenetic transgenerational trauma matrix unsettles the transparency of futurity, I also read micha cárdenas's transmaternity and transfuturity toward venturing into a more expansive landscape of nondeterministic potentiation.

Dilation acknowledges change and limitation, what are referred to as "cascades" within the soma between neurological and immunological activity. Dilation responds to immunological responses to stress in the form of trauma responses that travel through neural networks; dilation occupies this opportunity to address an individual truth while remaining attentive to a shared opportunity to care for shared truth in a manner that puts the social context of epidemiological exceptionalism in its proper spotlight. Change and limitation also describe the movement between body and environments, which the second and third chapters, "trauma" and "post/nation," accomplish in two degrees. Angel Dominguez's epistolary project *Desgraciado* presents our hemispheric history of colonialism as an intimacy with public vulnerability, and thus an unprocessed trauma, while in "post/nation" the nineteenth-century poet Albery Whitman's *The Rape of Florida* gives lyric form to a historical education on the American contract, consensus, and a settler-colonialism that the contemporary poet Demian DinéYazhí argues, poetically, is the post-apocalyptic reality that bonds intergenerational worldmaking.

Attending to the somatic-cognitive matrix creates, out of necessity, a style. Necessity is not the focus, however, and thus style here remains agnostic. But it is not amnesic. As such, each of these chapters intermixes my own personal analysis of experiences in America as a Central American immigrant, and part of the Salvadoran civil war diaspora. Through rather personal stakes in both the poetic and political analysis, I uncover the previously thought to be epigenetic heritability of trauma and maladaptive dysfunction to be less about personal, cellular deficit and, in fact, evidence of cultural-environmental plasticity and intergenerational experiences with the historical continuum of colonial exceptionalisms.

"Trauma is never a personal failure," Menakem reminds us. The anger poetry exhibits is braided to how lyric speakers testify to history as a territory existing between us as unique nervous systems belonging to a shared neurobiology. A territory over which migration and settlement, salvation and starvation have all unfolded an archive of bodily memories. The fourth chapter, "¡vecinos!" presents a generative poetics of negativity in the work of Douglas Kearney and Juno Morrow and situates contemporary poetics within the techniques and technology for archiving and mobilizing *aesthesis*.

I would add that, like trauma, anger is not a personal failure either, but rather a signal rippling from an unaddressed site of pain, or envy,[23] frustration, or resentment. Trauma, continues Menakem, is not "the result of someone's weakness, nor a limitation, nor a defect. It is a normal reaction to abnormal conditions and circumstances."[24] A poetry of anger is a poetry that responds to the "abnormal conditions and circumstances" of a transgression or pain, which is made abnormal either by an event's severity, permissibility, or fungibility or by an imbalanced recognition of truth, despite its apparent availability to be witnessed by an entire public. Purplishness produces anger in many bodies who are still trying to reclaim their consent, whose idea of justice begins with that. This is why I say that anger is a signal, and being open to its message is part of poetry's vatic register toward futurial possibilities for new descriptions of relation.

• • •

I am part of a diaspora community prompted by civil war, and our civil war was prompted by American intervention. I was born in El Salvador. We left when I was a few months old. My mother's body retained a great deal of distress around the time of my birth due to her parents' deaths and dispersal of her brothers across the globe as they ran from or toward comfort arising from the shared and sudden event of losing their foundation. My grandparents were run over by a car with US CONSUL plates in 1978, while walking home from having dinner with my parents and my then young brother. They were killed in front of many witnesses, yet there is no documentation confirming their deaths—and thus in a way their lives. There is no record except for the informally witnessed histories coalesced around the public event we are to understand never took place. The epigenetic context of being conceived in trauma, gestating in trauma, raised in the shadow of this experienced-unofficial past has conditioned my response to events in which my safety and the safety of bodies that look like mine or my parents' bodies, or little bodies that look like my kids' bodies, seem threatened in the fundamental way in which these bodies have been systemically denied public and political sentience. It's thought that trauma is a specific kind of thwarting of experienced time, and I mean experienced in the underdefined way of clumping together what we witness, desire, are told, and tell and retell ourselves after.

Biologically, evolutionarily, time is about life. This unsettles the necropolitical drive. In a consensus born historically in the beginnings of direct dehumanization, survival includes safety. Trauma is the experience of survival. In the post hoc analysis of phenomena, it is this after-the-event thinking that has led many to argue for a transgenerational understanding of certain kinds of heritable traumatic symptoms. As I ponder toward the end of the book, however, this heritable model is most likely not what is happening. Genes signal proteins, they don't manifest traits. What is of significance are the environmental, including cultural, conditions that generations share with each other in the sense of continued confrontations with power. Exceptionalism is a narrative wherein threats are coded with values specific to nationalized forms of supremacy. These are the very same acts of supremacy that many transgenerational communities have witnessed as violence. Anger, I posit, is an impassioned speech act toward shedding light on the shared trauma of being exploited by exceptionalism. Anger is derived from the personal experience of processing one's "reaction" to the dynamics of "abnormal" conditioning that describes the perceptible and subperceptible forces through which exceptionalism exacts its cultural influence. Anger, unique and singular to the body, spreads like fire. Poetry that demonstrates anger as the organizing force of its speech act directs its focus onto this power. It is liberatory and organizing simultaneously. It provides a safety, a duration wherein the cognitive center of our bodies is granted an opportunity to calm the reflexive, nervous network of our bodies. Menakem calls this the "soul nerve," but it is most often referred to as our vagus nerve. If we return to that wide horizon where the body, brain, and culture glow a most powerful and awe-inspiring color, the vagus nerve gathers the flocks of life fluttering between the shades and hues. It is the circuitry poetry arouses and indirectly addresses.

While my mother retained the distress of an experience cut short, the experience of having her parents get to know her children in an important chain of generational actualization, I have recycled the loop of expectation and void that resonates from the kind of trauma loss signifies. Mine are painful, many maladaptive and self-destructive, behaviors branching from the spontaneous and transient events of public death. But writing has given me permission to find resemblances in larger definitions of experience. The territory in between blossoms with rare dormant flowers that grow, nourished by the bacteria of the dead. This kind of sharing decenters my painful focus on one linear insecurity. It decolonizes the hold of exceptionalism on my right to find safety in caring and healthy ways that do not destroy the safety of others, or, as Menakem describes it, that "blow through others." Safety is a socialized fantasy that binds us to our human past, as political and technological creatures; anger is the remainder of this paradox, lived out with others.

My earliest memories of learning about my familial history and the death of my grandparents involves sitting in my mother's lap feeling her voice travel through my body. At the time, in my childish phenomenology, it was her utter magic that made feeling her voice possible. The person I am, a person restless in my own unrootedness and dysregulation, I have searched and searched only to learn that what made that stillness possible was the syncing and settling of our vagal systems. My temporal bone, the plate of calcium behind my ear and below the equator of my skull, rested on her breastplate. The vibrations of her voice rattled against this semidetached plate in my head, and together the two continents of our bodies created a humming, physical frequency that settled our nerves. Humming, singing, rubbing, these are all verified methods of treating the vagus nerve nowadays. We'd discovered gold, my mother and me. As I grew older our bodies shifted apart. But the memory and the history remained a part of our idiom. What I did not understand or appreciate was how settling our vagus also coded civic values through the content of her memories. Family, nation, migration, sadness, these also settled into the forefront of my brain and would tint all narratives with the expectation that people do "the right thing," or what it means when a nation is responsible for the lives of bodies that are not considered its "citizens." As I matured, I grew stressful, my body unstill. My body felt scared and threatened by the white-body supremacies I encountered, while my lizard brain made instinctual connections to the already existing trauma of death and diaspora instilled in me during early life.

Around the time of the pandemic, I started engaging with postmemory work, and reading about family systems theory and somatic abolitionism. It helped me understand that many practitioners engage with trauma at the epigenome, as an influence imparted onto children prior to consciousness, especially in diaspora communities effected by war.[25] I think the attraction to this approach is crafting an alternative model to the undeniable influence of social patterning. The epigenetic model of inherited trauma, in other words, confronts what I keep calling dilation, in that it underscores the vulnerability of imprinting and the operationalization of somatic imprinting in colonial-supremacist paradigms of assembly. Shared transgenerational traumas exist in a chain of affinities that the experience of national violence obscures with theoretical principles of right and wrong, deflecting the root of injury from structure to inheritance. On the one hand, this compartmentalizes therapeutic processes into digestible exercises individuals can engage in. But on the other, there is a missing step of orientation, which is what makes Menakem's approach of somatic abolition, in its framing of poetics between practice and address, so valuable to this project.

As I argue through the poetry, we recreate the scenes of untended trauma when the initial emotional signal is displaced from its social role as a message of event, as utterance. As neuroscientists have shown recently, the initial promise of "transgenerational trauma," as a therapeutic lens, is not a somatic cellular fact. Our cellular predisposition is most likely not being shaped according to affective histories. Yet, anger remains an important piece to understanding transgenerational experiences because it is each time a speech act that reflects living knowledge about the contemporary event of history from the unique perspectives of new witnesses to injustice. Braided together, we can trace the operationalization of social life as a conditioning of experience toward normalizing white-body supremacy at the expense of all other forms of living and definitions of democracy.

My transgenerational history of war begins in El Salvador and bleeds into the so-called war on immigration that defines my childhood and early adolescence in southern California. The Trump presidency revived that history in his COVID-era operationalization of a death-cultish obsession with health as an imaginary realm of eugenic supremacy and financial exceptionalism. My children's inheritance as mixed-race bodies will undoubtedly be that of racialization and sexualization. They will inherit the postapocalyptic disregard for all forms of earthly expenditure in the name of capitalism and exploitation. Their bodies will brace and their thoracic chambers will fold in on themselves, pinching veins and nerves, not because mine have, but because I haven't, with my generation, been able to do anything about the systemic colonialism that I was born into and leave behind. Despite my best efforts to yell ¡chicharros!

soma

> The largest part of your soul nerve goes through your gut, which has about 100 million neurons, more than your spinal cord. This is why we sense so many things in our belly—and why some biologists call the gut our "second brain." The second brain is where our body senses flow, coherence, and the rightness or wrongness of things.[1]

Menakem refers to the vagus nerve as the soul nerve, underscoring the role transmission plays in both trauma and soothing. I say soothing here and not healing because I want to hold off on the idea of finality when it comes to pain. I don't think it's impossible to "heal," but I'd like to explore an interstitial space between states, between the embodied knowledge of pain and the politicized need for being soothed. It's also important to note the different vectoral realities involved when the mind heals versus when the body heals, meaning there is an outward and an inward dilation or sense of time expression when each is considered. When an individual mind or a community of minds processes vast expanses of time toward settling disruption or conflict within, time is sensed to be at a standstill, calcified by pressures that creep into that space. The availability for a single body to breathe into that space, however, balloons into an expansiveness hyperbolically disproportional to the cultural banality demonstrated by the calcification of historical pain. The immediate, infinite relief of breathing into cultural stagnation cannot be understated. Conversely, healing a bone seems to take forever, even though the relative size of a fracture—the physical reality a fracture occupies in dimensional space—is small. The cellular time of replication, a phenomenon measurable in days, is finite and certain. Both models, however, signal a settling of the homeostatic state that organisms are hardwired to maintain. For many cultures, to be settled invokes an awareness of both times and directions. This is not the case, largely speaking, in the medical practices and therapeutics most likely to be insured in North America.

To be soothed or settled elicits, in our capitalist society, a need, and need is classified as an unwanted tax, an undesirable requirement that resources go to treat bodies that are ascribed value through value's own operational logics. There is a more dangerous chauvinism: the expectation that no one should feel homeostatic if what that requires is an interrogation of structures and institutions that permit only one group to feel the benefits of being settled. This is the eugenic cultural inheritance of our settler-colonial moral origins.

Bodies are profiled for being too preoccupied with trauma, labeled as being in too much of a deficit to be productive in a political sense, too pathological to participate in a sense of debate. Yet they remain exploitable in other forms that uphold the material foundations of the whole. Undesirability is a burden as well as an exploitable function that comes to envelop the identity of bodies that need.

These bodies are disqualified by capitalism, even while capitalism *needs* these bodies upon which to build its moralistic platform and reliance on expendability. Capitalism in this context of providing space for bodies operates as a system premised on exploiting disempowered bodies, on disempowering a body's magical demonstration of being alive, its drive to be soothed as a matter of homeostatic imperative. The imperative of "need" is thus broadly experienced through politicized rhetorics of a civic or common good. Healing is a demand that makes a eugenic assumption about the human body as "human capital stock."[2]

The soul nerve travels, searching within the bounds of our need to exist humanly. What happens to food under the eugenic assumption that politicizes need? What is poetry as a system of language that expends, demonstrates, and occupies spatiotemporality? Something happens in poetry that situates eating as a necessary activity that intersects with transgenerational and mnemonic soothing. And it's no coincidence that sometimes this demonstration is accompanied by degrees of frustration or anger over having to underscore the meaningfulness of this act.

Expectations that an individual heals from trauma shifts our cultural focus away from the processes that we might consider to be soothing, especially those that inspire communal well-being and the collective recognition that some things that have nothing to do with capitalistic morality feel good to our bodies. In a purely capitalist context, the individualization of the responsibility to heal makes sense. But the complex negativity surrounding hunger as need, or desire as hunger, and food as a repudiation of hunger through a richness of sensory, vagal communication tells us something about the dissatisfaction individuals and groups often feel toward the intersecting modes of systemic exploitation upon which capitalism builds itself. And so even if not about finance directly, poetry that engages with a lyric of soothing nervous centers can provide a blueprint for cultural change through introducing sensorial forms of syncing communal nervous responses to shared external environments. Food syncs our guts and our amygdala, our individual sense of calm and the community that provides that nourishment, the histories and landscapes from which flavors grow, and syncs our bodies to the hands that prepare it. When we eat we are communicating through our soul to other souls.

Soul wounds have commonly described the transgenerational and historical violence braided throughout Indigenous communities. Soul describes that which can be deeply hurt, but it also elicits an animation to the space-times that sit between. In the settler-colonial North American context space-times often imply objectivity and a passiveness waiting to be mapped and conquered. We are also conditioned to prioritize spatiality over temporality, which permits the agency of human involvement a maladaptive dominance over that which can be rationalized as existing for the benefit of the powerful. Those who can pretend they don't "need" because they benefit already from potential privileges that protect them from the world's sharp edges. The settler-colonial context, however, reveals its insecurities by its displacement of time in the desire to occupy quickly. Domination is an anxiety, while vulnerability opens to relation. If in the "second brain," as Menakem calls the vagal network, "senses flow" and "the rightness or wrongness of things," this to me describes its ability to ascribe timeliness as a measure of relation, not relation as the satisfaction of binary definitions: powerful versus powerless. What makes something "right" or "wrong" is often the kairotic nature of its arrival to a situation or condition of the felt. A hug is timely when you need it, stressful when touch is not wanted, for instance. Food, moreover, takes time. Eating reciprocates the temporal experience, completes it. Coherence is not a measure of knowledge, but the felt experience of knowing. And the alluring, soothing presence of food initiates its own timeliness by appealing to senses that anger, sadness, or hurt are not focused on. It soothes the sympathetic nervous system and triggers mnemonic images.

The space-time that sits between people and ancestors is a potentially active environment of collaborative imagination. They are also sites of exploitation where somatic need or dysregulation are heightened, named by supremacy, or even encouraged in a maladaptive manner.[3]

The seemingly objective space-time through which white-body supremacy rationalizes a dis/occupation of a caring kairos facilitates an intellectual and emotional retreat when one community is faced with the pain of another community and, rather than soothe them, dismisses their pain. One community experienced as dominant is encouraged to treat the space between it and others as a site for displaying power. For poets who engage in the vatic, those same interstices are cities of souls traveling, visiting, and sharing stories and soothing remedies. They are spaces of movement, contact. Poetry invokes them. Memory mobilizes them. Food in poetry invites souls and bodies alike, drawing them with the promise of nourishment. Bodies endure and talk to each other about love. They remember relationships, re-remember scenes wherein everyday events and objects acquire secondary meaning. And by the latter I mean more than symbolic or metaphorical meaning.

Re-remembering rehearses events that reach toward an emotional or hormonal charge. Engaging the parasympathetic nervous system, these rehearsals permit the body to complete a safety cycle without the direct presence of threat. Where the body might have fled, in the rehearsal the sympathetic nerves carry out a bolder future. Re-remembering permits memory to reconstruct a scene of love and safety, which serves the body in converting the cut-short nature of trauma with the coherence of an articulated self, a flow between generations and community.

There are two temporal dimensions here, which is why I call these poetics vatic. There is a futurity, which implies a safety not-yet materialized, and a present, which is the culminating experience of a historically material condition. Futurity is a matrix of possibilities attending to "condition," a sense of the body feeling forward, which has or is enduring politicized embodiment. It is a soothing without healing, an open-endedness. When healing is projected through the same body-exceptionalisms of normative American identity, namely able-bodied, cisgendered white-body supremacy, a supremacy of bodies that don't need to eat, that don't need to pause, cook, share, taste, remember, when healing is defined by this standard of a body-without-nerves, we are taught to prioritize competition for austere bundles of purchased care that attend to positional illnesses determined to be deserving or undeserving according to phobic cultural values.[4] We don't soothe one another. We measure pain and illness on the imaginary scales of moralized normativity and national productivity.

We never stop being angry, even when we experience joy. We never stop eating. There is no meal that satiates an organism that is constantly metabolizing and feeling the world. Futurity is always also about history, and about what we often call the structural, because in attending to the condition of the body futurity names the present as if it were an excavation of an iceberg revealing the profound roots frozen underneath what is visible. No one quite frames this as beautifully as José Esteban Muñoz, between queer futurity and Brown worlding. Queer futurity directs us toward ways of recognizing sovereignty via the very same institutions that deny personhood to queer embodiment, while "Brownness" includes "scopes of life" that resist and improvise from colonial histories. Food and the vagus nerve, as I feel them, are about this spatioemporal performance of a condition and a future, of memories and desire.

• • •

My friend Dorothy Chan writes the most amazing poems about food. I struggle to write about food because I am an addict. I don't have healthy memories about food that aren't also reminders that I never successfully got to know about my body without also inadvertently hurting it. I remember that I have consumed all manner of things that are not food, that were not prepared with hands intent on feeding a body, and this also hurts. Deep down I struggle with an anxiety that my desires for futurity might be perverted by what society deems to be deviant wants.[5] When I encounter negativity in poetry, however, there is knowledge there useful for advancement, for planning, and a counter-logistics to that which has been enforced upon us. "Hatpicality," Harney and Moten remind me, "the touch of the undercommons, the interiority of sentiment, the feel that what is to come is *here*."[6] Their sense of a space-time that is in front of us is a vital reminder to those of us with persistently anxious thoughts: a persistently haptic need to be settled. Hapticality is a perception of touch, but touching is itself not necessary because the intention to *feel* others is the desire that defeats the learning of isolation, atomism, and the exploitation of others as a self-defensive survival strategy. It's the "capacity to feel through others, for others to feel through you, for you to feel them feeling you," a vulnerability and a relationality that recognizes the shared status of dispossession. The original dispossession is a dispossession from our own selves as sites of care.

I have felt from time to time that, for reasons of dominance and supremacy, the soothing I need is fundamentally not American. To demonstrate this need in public would be a terroristic demand for resources that my body is not entitled to. My food poems are so weakened by my anxiety to be public about my dysfunction that I even took a class with Dorothy once at our public library, hoping that writing in public with others would help. What I learned from them is this: food offers an improvisational expanse of options and sensations that permit the body to complete its want, to blow through contexts that attempt to thwart that original need, which is love. Love includes getting to know the unique way collective, familial pain settles into my own body, at least seemingly so. This epigenetic possibility, and it is maybe just a possibility, was never given equal space to locating my family's trauma in the known narratives that circulated around the dinner table, which by extension included pre-prescribed religious rubrics, or communal responsibilities. As limited as my experiences with process have been, food remains a palpable medicine. Medicine, however, also circulates in our settler-colonial inheritance, politicized in competitive markets referred to as "health." Those who know haptically improvise through the synesthesia available in the felt, as a bypass to vagal soothing. Resmaa Menakem situates the central metaphor of somatic abolitionism in his learning both history and soothing from his grandmother's embodied reality, the testimony her body demonstrates. We begin with the somatic and explore meaning and purpose in flavor and memory.

> My grandmother was a strong and loving woman. But her body was frequently nervous. She often had a sense that something terrible was about to happen. It was an ancient, inherited sensation that rarely left her—a traumatic retention.
>
> . . .
>
> She also frequently comforted herself by rocking, both forward and backward and from side to side. When I would watch her rock, it never looked nervous or neurotic. Instead, it felt like a sacred ritual, imbued with meaning and purpose.[7]

One might wonder what love has to do with anger. The answer is the body. Love can be a strategy against systemic minimization. Love makes us big, expansive. Love reminds us of networks and journeys that our present condition or situation obscures. Love is "*here*" as Harney and Moten might say. Love occupies space in a way that clears the room for our bodies to take it up. "I wonder about how food and love / go hand in hand," begins one of Dorothy Chan's sonnets in their series "Dream Menu Sonnets."[8] This, after the first two in the series in Chan's *Revenge of the Asian Woman* (2019), reminisces on postmemories, turning at the site of food to disclose the desires of her yet-to-be parents. "Back in the eighties in Hong Kong, my dad is on the train / with a Big Mac and fries and a ten-count nugget meal," begins the first sonnet in the series, with McDonalds signaling a transnational love language that makes domestic promises between early lovers, intent on eating up the world between them as a shortcut to closeness. "McDonalds was the crème de la food for co-eds from Kowloon, / the crispy flavor of America—the dream," marking this moment with a giddiness, a euphoria that in the first sonnet is innocent and *norm*.[9] The second in the sequence, however, begins to define a queerness in this puppy-love narrative and a substantial age difference between them. Difference around desire, love, and satisfaction builds throughout the series (and Chan's work) to claim the queerness of the poetic speaker themself and the felt difference in how they eat and claim space for a body that must, like all other bodies, eat. Chan's queer poetics is the *hereness* of a body that is on-time, that is not a memento of a nostalgia or a space traveler from some speculative future. "My mother's pretty happy right at that moment—" a *rightness* as a right-on-timeness to the food as love. That is, "right at the moment of laughing harder, / shutting the door on my father's face, / because no boys allowed, / actually no men allowed, my mother at twenty, my father at thirty-four."[10]

I want to think about transnational love, queer love, Brown love, and the spatiotimeliness of wanting. "Sometimes she let us grandkids sit on her lap as she rocked," continues Menakem from the quote above. "When I close my eyes, I can still feel my body settling into her soft, thick arm holding me steady and safe across her chest, and the wavelike motion of being rocked, of becoming part of a flow." For those of us who are part of diaspora communities, our grandmother's bodies were not readily available growing up. I mention this because admittedly there is a window when a body fits in another body, and

I know this from the experience of holding my children in my lap—literally becoming furniture for their bodies. Holding them and not letting go. Feeling our breathing in and out of sync, not becoming one but syncing as two. We have improvised toward touching time through this syncing in a desire to know that our feeling a need for affirmation is a valid soothing activity that binds us to those who have invested so much of their lives for our future happiness, our future loves.

For those of us in diaspora we have turned to proxies. Some of us, lost in systems of disembodied capitalisms, have turned to shadows of proxies that have not truly soothed us even if they filled us. Food is a proxy because it involves memory and the haptic in ways very similar to those that soothe the vagus nerve, and it actually occupies space and time. We go out and eat the foods that soothe, reach for them. Hands prepare this food. People live off this food. Being in the presence of certain foods heightens our proprioception. They embody in their flavors and colors what we want. We are public in this eating. Our want is made public and made known. Eating causes changes in the microbiota of our gut, sparking a signal in the brain.[11] Diaspora sickness can be reached through an intentional cataloguing of flavors that trigger specific memories. We reach out in our environment for plates and flavors that revisit and rehearse original pains and love for the purpose of reexamination. This endurance between imagination and metabolism describes a lot of Chan's work: "Orgasms of food and Picasso painting in front of us."[12] It describes some of my sites of self-harm. They have been, also, attempts at reaching out to others. Attempts at articulating, through my body, a want that my speech has not had a place to name.

"Give me everything I want, is probably what my mother / was thinking at age twenty in her college dorm, / waiting for my father to show up with McDonald's," begins the tenth in the series.[13] It's a reservation the poetic speaker eschews. The excess in Chan's sonnets, including the excess of voltas throughout, which braid the sonnets into the "story" they write for themselves, speak. The speaker claims space in an environment where what appears expansive around them, America, is really plastic décor. Fake. Homophobic.

> . . . America
> is too afraid of anything that's gay, I think about
> what it would be like to be someone's beloved,

and how everyone wants to claim somebody, but why,
   and sure, I'll wear a sparkling choker in the bedroom,
but don't you dare give me a leash in real life.[14]

Chan's sonnets are *methetic* and participatory in a way recipes themselves are, gaining and losing details as communities carry them to different countries, translate them, look tirelessly for impossible-to-find ingredients under the pale fluorescent lights of giant box stores. "Brownness is an efficacious alternative" to terminologies and taxonomies of difference "because it permits us to think about how some people's sense of brownness may potentially touch other people's sense of brownness."[15] While Muñoz may not be thinking explicitly of familial Brownness, for many diaspora communities, second and third generation descendants inevitably must improvise how they ask to be soothed from what's available. Queer kids also inevitably stretch identities across conservative roots and expansive communities through food, as if floating on cartoon hands made of smells. The touching-knowing Brownness is a *methexis* that connects families across oceans and territories, and rather than define any one manner of love, it soothes the bumps and schisms of what can be improvised.

Menakem's description of being soothed by his grandmother, literally soothed by being given permission to "settle" into her body, moreover, illustrates the performative power in what Muñoz has called Brownness, which informs the converging space-time of love between the poets I'm reading, in that they occupy and demonstrate landscapes of somatic and politicized experience: "Brownness is vast, present, and vital. It is the ontopoetic state . . . of a majority of those who exist, strive and flourish within the vast trajectory of multiple and intersecting regimes of colonial violence."[16]

Sometimes those "intersecting regimes" are apparitions between generational memories within the same transnational, Brown, or queer families. "My grandmother hates it when I wear black," opens Chan's "Triple Sonnet for Good Boys, Grandma's Cookies, and Girls with Their Cream Cheese and Lox." To wear black is "not what good Chinese girls do / to their ancestors or to the good Chinese boys / who take you home to family dinner."[17] When readers engage with BIPOC and QTPOC poets who write through food, there may be a misconception about the kinds of joy caloric nihilism or flavor abundance present. And it's a misconception about expansiveness and joy, really. Joy isn't exceptionally the state of sadness's absence, and expansiveness isn't a state free of borders. Joy is love in the presence of melancholia, or loss, distance, or disillusioning realities. Expansiveness isn't achieved without some heartbreak and pain that comes from spatialism. Expansiveness directs our attention to the borders that seek to govern where bodies are meant to stay and who gets to move freely.

I read Brownness as an intersectional worlding that builds off Muñoz's work on queer futurity, queerness "in the horizon, forward dawning and not-yet-here,"[18] as a futurity that simultaneously unsettles the expected cisnormative domination over nonbinary identities as a relationship that permits a grasping that is knowledge and embodied at once: knowledge as a window into the violence freely articulated in space, as a sort of reiterative exhale of manifest destiny mapped onto the soma as if it were a universal projection. Brownness requires touching, particularly "comprehension through surface touching."[19] This is not the same as domination-as-mastery, or mastery-qua-domination, but I think of it rather as the surface touching that produces vagal frequencies, a touching that is transgenerational in presenting dishes as mnemonic proxies of our families, homes, and journeys. This touching soothes because it is a receiving. A surface touching reminds bodies of their place in a cycling braid of ancestors, medicines, and recipes.

• • •

After earning my MFA I was living in a Los Angeles neighborhood of hipsters and Salvadoreños. I was both, coincidentally. Being poor, restless, and hungry, I would spend my evenings walking up and down Sunset Boulevard, smelling food and looking into windows. The Pentecostal faith is very popular throughout our hemisphere largely because it translates the Bible into languages beyond the Spanish-English binary. I would speculate that a lot of it also has to do with the music. The Salvadoreño Pentecostal churches—on Sunset, and along Santa Monica Boulevard, up and down the Los Feliz corridor, and deep into Pico down toward the 10, along which I'm sure someone could map the music and gritos from the Pacific to Juárez—they are a lively place to be. On Sunset, west of downtown and east of Sunset Junction, many of these churches are in storefronts with large adjacent spaces like parking lots, or they encroach on their commercial neighbors like autobody shops. The churches set up immense griddles the likes of which I've only ever seen at sidewalk pupuserias in San Salvador. Pupusas outside, gritos inside. And the music is jamming, with that kind of thump you feel when the drummer's foot kicks down as if jumping up stone steps to space. They are pretty barebones, these bands. Drums, voice, guitar, sometimes bass. An organ that takes care of it all if it's just two up there singing and moving. The players and singers are sometimes related. You walk into the room and there's an unmistakable brow or nose or cheekbone stretching across the sweaty faces on stage, each a portrait of the same face at different ages.

When I first encountered one of these churches I remember standing at the edge of the sidewalk. There was a track for a large sliding metal gate and I remember my forefoot draped over the metal and feeling the music in my toes. I was invited in by a woman behind the pupusas. She waved a plate at me smiling a smile, and I had no choice but to smile back at and step toward the music.

If you've ever had a pupusa, a good one, you know they go down way too easy for something with so much in them you really shouldn't be eating. By this time in my life, I'd made my decision about religion. The last mass I'd attended was with my grandparents in El Salvador, and I was maybe twelve. And yet, there was a small chapel in Newhall, California, near my graduate school, that I used to visit from time to time, just sitting inside between services. I wouldn't pray. Maybe I was meditating. I was just taking a break. In any case, I love live music, and pupusas took me home. I am not religious, but I grew up in a religious home. When my grandmother was dying recently, I appreciated how religion allowed people to approach my family, whereas the smell of mortality often keeps the timid away from mourners in North America, afraid of the uncomfortable reminder that we are not as invincible as we have been led to believe. Religion is a way into a space that honors how sometimes a friend just needs company while they cry and reminisce. Belief or faith, or muscle memory, whatever it actually is, allowed people from all degrees of separation from my grandmother to offer us comfort through written phrases and references to god.

I understand the history and present practices of Pentecostalism. But as a poet I am enamored by the magic of all speech acts. I am partial to the idea that maybe there are aesthetic patterns innate to our evolutionary selves that rise to the surface in moments of ceremony, usurping the artificial patterns and rhythms of daily life under capitalism. And sometimes that ceremony attends to the unavailable. I don't wish to make light of my brief time in these churches because something was happening in them that is still happening right now, human endurance fueled by pupusas. A rapture that brings bodies close to something that only permits proximity and not occupation; a rapture that permits knowing but not possessive knowledge; a rapture interrupted by the kindness of folks handing out pupusas—it's an endurance that carries a price of admission, sweat. Pupusas are the fuel. As I have said, I am an addict. Filling my body or my abdomen specifically to a physical limit to where my tissue has no choice but to press against my vagal nerves, like hostages stuffed into a container that ballons at the top from the escape of toxins, this was my display in a faith that was not allowed to exist in any other space or time as a social or political body. I felt held in the bodily funk of a small room with expending bodies that had spent all week already laboring away, tiring. But this was about soothing. And the pupusas provide a thick yellowy fat that burns like whale oil. I had during this time in my life, the early 2000s, no health insurance. I had virtually no resources. I worked as contingent labor in higher ed, but never with enough contractual security to access care. I desired to be soothed.

To ask for help is seen today as an act of holding America hostage. Asking for help is disqualified as a demonstration of political activism. Individually, atomistically, we consume. Eating in the presence of those neighbors who are still out there shouting and cooking and inviting in strangers was like no other experience I've had with food.

• • •

Food gives us permission to love ourselves in a space and time shared with others, whether at the table or behind a partition where the food was prepared. Food is love, a soothing that takes place in the gut. Gurgling contractions massage our vagal epicenters. Food being love itself, when we encounter it in poetry by BIPOC or QTPOC poets we are asked also to consider the trauma nourishment soothes. This poetry, entangled in acts of eating up, being eaten up, burning fat, cooking up elements, is as much about food as it is about the persistence of systems. Sensed in our vagal epicenter, poetic food is transmitted into the lyric mitochondria and vessels throughout the community invited to the table.

Take Elizabeth Alexander's "Butter," for example. "My mother loves butter more than I do," the speaker announces, "more than anyone. She pulls chunks off / the stick and eats it plain."[20] Then begins traveling the gut-memory network through the dishes and events where butter and life braid over and across each other, colors, aromas, and sensations marking where the two graze each other and press into one another. Moments of "butter melting in small pools in the hearts / of Yorkshire puddings, butter better / than gravy staining white rice yellow." "When I picture / the good old days I am grinning greasy," they remember.

Whenever I see mention of "the good old days" my shoulders raise up to my ears in a self-defensive bracing for that American nostalgia reminiscing on days when violence was given full range of social movement.[21] Violence is never far from the scene of eating butter throughout Alexander's poem, either. But also it is never given the authority over sensation. Her mother loving butter "more than I do" is her mother's memory and generational proximity to mid-century America and Jim Crow policies and practices. Lasting into the 1960s, butter is the speaker's love, also. Learned love, love as knowledge, and acquainted through the meals that describe a daily interaction at the table, in the kitchen, between flavors. Invoking the "good old days" is the stitching act, or braiding, which for many American communities better describes temporality as constantly returning to the material evidence of withstanding, as opposed to nostalgia as the fictive reiteration of old exceptionalisms. Butter is the fat the body burns in its steady state of metabolic survival, of *endurance*. Butter exists in a state of triglycerides interlocked together waiting to be converted into energy, burned like the last light in a barren welcomeless landscape. Melted, it can be frozen. Frozen, it can be melted. Fried, it releases a unique flavor that one smells first, coating stove tops and walls with a residue reminder. The unique flavor of burning butter is a magic, an aurora borealis of fat and non-fat components touching in the atmosphere of a kitchen. Baked into yeast and flour, its methyl ketones and lactones crisp into a sweetness.

You can eat butter the same, in any state. You can "pull chunks off / the stick," you can eat it "plain." Joy isn't the absence of sadness. Abundance isn't the absence of threat. My dad used to eat butter. We'd go to Sizzler, and he'd eat the little squares. He'd spread it cold on bread with tomato in the middle of the night. My mother revealed to me once that he started doing this when we first came to the US, and he'd sit on the corner of the bed in the middle of the night eating this weird sandwich. I imagine the brightness of tomato and the dull earthy sweetness of fat kind of mushing together in his mouth and becoming wet bread. He also has night terrors. It's anxiety. It's Menakem's grandmother singing her body into calmness, rocking herself. Licking butter and syrup off a plate gives you those magical deep brown calories that live in your blood and settle between muscle fibers like droplets of glass in a stage somewhere between fragility and melt. Anyone with a bag of deeply yellow-brown breast milk in the freezer knows exactly how fat is life.

Butter in its molecular plasticity, in its mitochondrial syrup, is the medium of a return and futurity, a future based on what needs addressing now, from what has been. Violence is never gifted authority, but that doesn't mean Alexander refuses to rescript it as relational, as generational. This poetic movement through sensation, not the authority of violence, is the forward momentum heightened in the verb tense itself, "I *am* grinning greasy / with my brother, having watched the tiger / chase his tail and turn to butter. We *are* / Mumbo and Jumbo's children." Butter is the coal in the engine that whistles *I am* into all dimensions. In referring to Helen Bannerman's children's story, "Little Sambo" (1899), Alexander places her act of eating and the power of butter directly in the American jungle where to exist is to be hunted. To shine is to be seen by predation. And so, if you're going to be seen you best be glowing hot like the fire from the sun, from the earth's very core. In Bannerman's story "Little Sambo's" parents, "Mumbo" and "Jumbo," lovingly provide their child with most exquisite clothes, which various tigers along LS's path take in exchange for not eating LS. In the end, and after LS has traded items of clothing for staying alive, all the tigers thirsty for dominance-as-power take the items of clothing they've acquired from LS off and bite each other's tails, going round and round until they've consumed themselves and metabolized ghee, Indian clarified butter. LS picks up the clothes and puts them all back on. The father, walking home, stumbles upon the large puddle of ghee and collects it in a jar for dinner. Together the family eat the metabolized tigers.

There are competing economies of power, ghostlike, in Alexander's poem, among them the cannibalism of the anthropomorphic tigers who conceptualize the value of haberdashery in an exchange market, and the power passed down by the speaker's mother's love for butter—her passing down of a knowledge that butter provides a valuable nourishment for the environment the children in the poem are being raised in. "We *are*" is an affirmation, but also an anxiety. While "glowing from the inside" can be romanticized as a force, for many parents it might also be a worry that their kids remain visible and vulnerable—not visible and recognized—that they are illuminated, even, in this condition between indignity and recognition. A spotlight is cast on them and thus they become detectable by predators. "One hundred megawatts of power" in this complicated turn fits into what would be Alexander's later writing on how to survive through a spectacular visibility, or what she terms the "agglomerating spectacle" of public death.

> I call the young people who grew up in the past twenty-five years the Trayvon Generation. They always knew these stories. These stories formed their world view. These stories helped instruct young African Americans about their embodiment and their vulnerability. These stories were primers in fear and futility. The stories were the ground soil of their rage.[22]

Trauma lives in the body. This is the premise of transgenerational trauma. But it needs parsing. Trauma lives in the body in the sense that trauma is a response, articulated somatically, to our environments. Trauma lives in our body the way violence lives in our environment. Living in a body refers to ongoing processes like the cascading signals that translate into sensory memory and imagistic archives of experiences in the world. As a phrase, living in the body recognizes something human. I refer to transgenerational trauma, for now, as the reflexes and speed and the instinctual desires to stay safe in America. But there is more to discover about the somatic-cognitive dynamic when it comes to generation and trauma, which I get to later.

The Trayvon Generation is a generation in a state of anxiety. This anxiety under the cumulous cloud of digital memory and social media algorithms becomes a collective organism. An assembly affected by the contagion of spectacularized, which is to say normalized and banalized, death. "I worry about this generation of young [B]lack people," continues Alexander. She worries because she is also a mother, and she worries about depression in young people. Depression is a disillusionment at the hormonal level and caregivers worry about despondency and constant, mysterious illnesses, and eventually a deep toxic anger that is like a poison against brightness. Alexander ultimately is writing about the "[B]lack creativity that emerges from long lines of innovative responses to the death and violence that plague" the Black community. That innovation not only abolishes somatic retention through the speech act, but also draws attention to the source of trauma in a manner that maps the work that needs doing in other present bodies toward resolving retained anger, depression, or felt inadequacy in the comparative existence of real bodies within the systemic white-body supremacy that defines American culture.

Eating is about survival, but in the story of LS, eating is also about supremacy and domination. Eating is about love and generational holding. What we eat is about learning which foods give your body sustenance in times of need. Eating can also be cannibalistic, and irrational—the kind of eating-of-others that describes a lot of colonial and settler-colonial experiences. There is a nihilism at work in the eating that poets embrace as a hyperbolic attentiveness to the felt event that unfolds after, which is metabolized into language. This hopping from one material physics to another is important. The synesthetic wiring between body and speech draws knowledge from the paradox of democratic contradiction. It's vital that folks who *feel* something under democracy are understood as also *knowing* something about what they feel, and possibly why they feel it. How it works to feel. Walter Mignolo calls this returning "sentience" to the subjects of colonial history. Mitochondrial adaptation is at the center of how we understand fat as a vital energy source, a clean and level energy, for lack of a better description, in that it doesn't produce the same levels of lactic byproduct. Though we understand the cerebral need of lactic acid for the maintenance of membrane health, lactic byproduct, nonetheless, is associated with high musculoskeletal output, and thus demand beyond supply. The body in a state of endurance is a body in control of its expenditure—*in control*. In control of oneself.

Then your dad comes home with a jar of ghee and there's a party on. I want to rethink what poetry is in relation to the party. What's served sparks an opportunity to seize upon what's going on. We feel the drumkit and smell the fat through our skin. When I read poems about food, I feel through them and remember that some of us are valued less than others in America. And I am reminded that raising this issue in front of others doesn't always yield the intended result, which is asking others to care that this is so. Sometimes one is even accused of causing trouble for doing this.

• • •

> When your body feels relaxed, open, settled, and in sync with other bodies, that's your soul nerve functioning.[23]

As Menakem goes on to explain, however, when the body feels restricted in anyway, threatened, or insecure, those are also vagal nerve functions. One might say that the primary, evolutionary purpose of the vagal nerve is to govern our fight, flee, or freeze response. This response, while seemingly instantaneous and a matter of reflex, is a communicative process between the vagus nerve and our amygdala, or lizard brain as it's often called. Insecurity, unsettledness, or disruption in our vagal nerves sends a message to the amygdala, which responds in one of the aforementioned actions: fight, flee, or freeze. These responses, as signals, are spread across executive functions throughout the whole of the body. Instantaneousness is an important sense of reaction. The quicker, the more subperceptible actions seem, the more secure a body feels in its capacity to survive.

We focus on our fight, flee, or freeze responses because, in many ways, these are the responses that have kept human bodies alive throughout evolutionary history. Speed, however, is also an echo of the performance capitalism that fuels masculine panic's outward aggression toward other bodies. And what I'm trying to draw out is pacing. Slowness. There are, certainly, many historically anthropological contexts wherein threats and fear would be considered biological imperatives: predation, starvation, overexposure. But this does not mean that love responses or care responses have been any less vital in the evolutionary story of humankind.

Over time, what's happened to love? Love is a powerful force, as powerful as fear when it comes to how our bodies function. When bodies feel "energized, vibrant, and full of life, that's also your soul nerve," Menakem reminds us. We've given cultural priority to survival as physical securitization and have permitted the eradication of threats to homogeneity through quick violence. But the vagus nerve serves "another purpose," one that is "precisely the opposite: to receive and spread the message of *it's okay; you're safe right now; you can relax.*" The timeliness here is also important. Love and care can be reflexes. They can be responsive, instinctually communicated through embodied nervous systems.

Joshua Nguyen has a butter poem too: "TOAST / BUTTER / SUGAR / HAIBUN." It's a poem about spreading the signal, "it's okay; you're safe right now; you can relax." But, as in this passage, it's also a poem about changing the context of an environment overdefined by stimulation or, in other words, by direct signals to the nerves—changing an absence of control response to a love response, a powerlessness response to a safety response:

> ... My room is the game room. My room can't block out
> any sound. I can't sleep even with all my pillows squeezed against my
> ears. But my mother, in between love songs & songs about war & songs
> I couldn't place, comes upstairs to see how I am coping. *You know
> what you could make us tonight* ... she says, caressing my face. My eyes
> widened, excited. *You can even use the white bread!*

My parents had wild parties while I was growing up. We also had a karaoke machine. The parties were usually on Fridays, and people came from Tijuana where my dad worked. After a long week they would come over to our house, and I knew my dad's car would be filled with pounds and pounds of meat, tortillas, friends, and we had coolers of beer already filled with ice. I knew coming home from school the backyard would be smelling like green onion grilling and carne asada. As night fell and the grill glowed, and the bottles and plates littered in the dusk like stars and dwarf planets, the asada would enter a more apostrophic phase, an "embarrassing" phase to use Culler's description of poetic disclosure.

Nguyen's use of the haibun is a way of dealing with memory. All of the poets I read here are dealing with memory, to be clear. The haibun is traditionally a prose-haiku, bringing together the epiphanous economy of haiku with the situated grammar of prose. Matsuo Bashō's seventeenth-century *Narrow Road into the Interior* is one of the earliest examples of haibun. Its haiku elements underscore the Buddhist worlding Bashō witnesses in the momentous and fleeting experience of detail, much like those experiences of my border universe, wherein the infinite demonstrated itself in the everyday smallness of details I felt only I noticed while looking away from a public that made me anxious and craving tomato and butter sandwiches. Prose elicits movement and heterogeneity of experience. Prose grammar reiterates the approachable reality of existing in the midst of worlding; it is language both moved by the scenery and moving the scenery along. Prose's breadth and ebb permits human embodiment its curiosity, its metabolism, allows a poetics to fatigue, and migration. In other words, prose is our restlessness. The humanity always aspiring to the full thoughtfulness of Zen. It's at peaceness. As Nguyen explains:

... once you reflect on the memory multiple times, it can change depending on higher feeling, what music you are listening to, etcetera, which is just a lesson in perspective and a lesson in seeing all sides or every minutia of something, even a memory.... When you recall a story to someone, you do not tell every little thing; you still curate some of it to an extent.[24]

The men always tried for the boleros. With their shirts tucked-in uncomfortably to their '90s jeans, and their masculinity belied by big cartoonish white sneakers, they would close their eyes and summon their best Vicente Fernandez. I think about the line in Nguyen's haibun, "My uncle grabs the micro- / phone. He's not reading the room well—chooses a song about two lovers who try to find each other / in the midst of war—they don't. My uncle sweats symphonies."

There was a performance I don't think I fully appreciated then, how people were maybe asking to be heard, and their story be heard. I can remember this detail now because of my own migrations. I see now their performance was a story about how they got there. How they'd made it through a week of sweating in a hot factory, and how they had desires that pressed against limits. How their environments framed those limits according to moral hieroglyphics intersecting with learned narratives about their bodies, narratives they'd had no say in composing but unwittingly proliferated through performance. How the men had experienced growing into their masculinity "so close to the United States, yet so far from god."[25] The men all admired each other silently, then laughed at each other. Kind of like a verbal ¡chicharros! As Jonathan Culler wrote, "Apostrophe works to constitute a poetic speaker taking up an active relationship to a world or element of the world constructed as addressee, an addressee which is often asked to respond in some way, as if the burden of this apostrophic event were to make something happen."[26]

When you grow up contextualized by the politics of recognition you read Jonathan Culler and get caught up in little theoretical details like this. "Addressee" sticks out, for example, because there is an implication of a body in space in relation to another. And if the body exists in space, how does it feel there? Safe? Threatened? Devalued? Dignified, entitled to be there? Behind the term there is a landslide of memories, of myself being addressed. Especially

FIGURE 4. Friday, Nestor, California, 1990 something.

in public. They are not entirely positive, though some of them are memories of love. What does it mean to "make something happen"? Have we not been making things happen? Let's make something happen then! We eat. We cook. We share pupusas. We remember as an act of poetic speech, and it can't help but split like dry wood twisted too suddenly, one address to "an active relationship to a world," the other a direct address to the mnemonic figures and specters that in equal measure trigger messages across the spectrum of our nerves.

I understand I'm being literal to the point of stalling the argument. That's the point about politics as an intersection of thought and action. If we aren't literal about the bodies at stake in the care that politics is meant to focus on, then we give implicit consent to a universal concept of the body, a universal addressee. Whose memories do we fill its head with? The universal subject is an artifice of dominant supremacy, and, as a privileged citizen of that universe, that it would fight to "make something happen" is suspect. And if it were to do so, I worry about what that universal address would fight to make happen. Different folks can love each other, nonuniversal beings in fact. They can dance together. Embarrassingly even.

The women always sang in groups, and they sang lively songs, dance songs. I remember their hair, saturated in so much aerosol I'm surprised no one ever caught on fire. They moved in improvised choreography as they sang. They laughed together. Unlike Nguyen's speaker, I experienced these sounds with my brother. It was mitigated through his eyes and ears as much as mine. My brother was a toddler when we came to the US and was fully verbal. I wonder how that inflected his needs at that time. He would have been aware of material limits, material changes. Changes to the environment, the steep green streets and bird orchestras replaced by expanses of an endless brown-yellow ground made wavy by radiant heat and cricket drone. He would've noticed the new insects, giant antlike things called niños de la tierra, and the horrible cactus plants everywhere. There's a picture of me singing myself happy birthday with my big cheeks full of cake. I'm standing on the table, maybe exhibiting the impulsiveness that was to come, and my brother is sitting in a chair and looks kind of sad. Kind of like he's an adult and was just laid off or failed to get into college. My needs were put out like wildfire with big hugs and holding, or my Winnie the Pooh blanket. I wonder, today, how maybe his having language made certain kinds of physical love not as meaningful. Nevertheless, a relationship to food is a darkness we share.

> . . . My mother hits a high note—the words on-screen scroll from white to blue—it is so loud here. The window to apply butter is getting smaller.

> . . . I grab the butter from the fridge & with no knife in sight, I smush the fat & protein between my fingers—fingernails turning bronze—open the toaster oven door & wipe my buttered hands over the toast.[27]

There is one thing that resonates fully with Nguyen's memory, for me. One had no choice, as a child. Something opens when I read Nguyen's haibun, a "constitution" that verifies the subjective memory of my experiences and that of myself as an audience member of his reaching poetic address. Everything underneath this aurora where the two meet like gases takes on clearer definition, for me *now*. Me, within my context of terms and motivations, the particular dopamine curve I experience, like a bell or singing bowl. A "world" is constructed in witnessing the power of this act of memories and how bodies are witnessed caring for each other through nourishment. Bodies claim their space through their desires, witnesses learn from witnessing, and this is truly powerful when that knowledge sustains the energy to survive genocide as a form of politics. A politics that does not recognize universal addresses but only the unique voices that fight to make something happen. Worlding is a validation of the verbiage, gives "make" a direction and definition in the experiential "happen." Worlding is upheld only in so long as *we* feed it. Worlding eats memories and expended acts of soothing.

If my brother and I were lucky, there would be other kids at these parties, and we could make it work. Most often though we were an island in a tempest of off-tones and encouraging whistles. We would go into my parents' room and turn the TV up really loud, our version perhaps of squeezing pillows against our ears. No one ever checked on us, though. We'd hear clumsy footsteps and laughter as people stumbled to the bathroom. The kitchen was our Switzerland. When I'd hear my mother's voice, I'd sneak to the kitchen to see what food she was bringing in. She'd put it before me and I'd eat it like a fox, carrying away the last bites to my den aglow with screen light. I get so much of what Nguyen recounts, as if reading a travel narrative of a place not unlike my origins. I understand what it's like to feel disempowerment like a thunder, in your parents and in the adults around you, through their affect and through a specific kind of joy that is love in the face of something else, something more complicated, but any one other thing in a binary sense. You hear thunder before you feel lightning, but it's already all happening no matter what or where you locate yourself in relation. I know what powerlessness feels like in a storm moving across the people you resemble or rely on. I have also, despite the hormonal storm inside my brain surrounding pleasure-seeking and addiction, remained connected to motivation. What does this have to do with anything, one might ask?

The vagus nerve, the "soul nerve," as Menakem prefers to call it, is more than an emotional-nervous processing center, "It's where we feel a sense of belonging." It is thus both an embodied "organ" and "a communal one."[28] This is where culture plays an interesting role. In recent history, neurobiologists have debunked the pleasure-principle thinking surrounding dopamine. I'm thinking of the work of Dr. Robert Malenka's lab on plasticity and dopamine, which posits that neural reward circuitry plays a large role in prosocial behaviors that can be thought of in the context of environmentally intricate survival.[29] I bring this up to ponder the situation of supremacy experienced as a kind of spectacularized, banalized violence, including one projected through media onto the surfaces of our haptic surroundings. Do these signals disrupt the dopaminergic reward circuitry tied to group-survival via prosocial adaptive behaviors? I raise this concern because not all bodies will respond to this stimuli with the same neural-immunological needs, given that white bodies might in fact find quick access to social acceptance and dopaminergic rewards through sensations of belonging. It's a far more complicated exchange along neural pathways and involves our cortex in a narrative manner that produces a feedback loop. Our subjective experiences surrounding an activity animate the dopamine curve. In a larger environmental context, what happens when the subjective experience that creates the enjoyable feeling of belonging is entangled with historical power, and the ways power frames belonging according to positional categories, like race, gender, ability, region, property? I've been looking at how lyric acts attach themselves to food, where food blossoms environmentally within a social mnemonic. Lyric acts, in this context, map the neural pathways toward a jouissance of belonging, even if there are potentially negative memories or contexts surrounding the timeliness in realizing that one belongs.

Joshua Nguyen has spoken about the complexity of BIPOC writers engaging with food, for instance, noting how when composing his book *Come Clean* (2021),

> I was thinking about food and foodways and how a lot of the food writing people turned me to, or food writing I read is romanticized, which I think has its place. And I am grateful for it because it has helped me like connect with my Vietnamese, my Asian heritage, but because I worked in the kitchen and I have seen my mom stressed out over food, and I have seen the chef I worked with like get super stressed over food.[30]

When I was coming of age as a young writer in the early 2000s I really felt food writing to be a problematic site. Food writing by immigrant writers especially was consumed by a general audience, while immigrant bodies themselves were discarded. Or consumed themselves as labor. "Food," continues Nguyen, can also direct us to the love in that labor, as when he reminisces on food and his relationship to his mother. Food can also be "a medium to talk about the gaze, who is consumed, and who is the consumer." There is nothing idyllic about soothing. For many bodies that have experienced feeling settled in the calmer body of another, or have felt the coherence of belonging, there is a recognition, but also, a caution toward feeling displayed. You can feel like you belong; that doesn't mean you "matter." Mattering is a self-esteem desire projected onto how an assembly values its members or doesn't. How it misses individuals when they're missing from the whole or doesn't. What is public is the example of relation, not the disclosure of internal turbulence settled in the available labor of another. The latter is what we call spectacularization, which creates a fungible spectacle out of emotional expenditure for the sake of entertaining an idealized audience that completes the narrative cycle of human exhaustion without having to actually seek out the fulfilling dopamine curve of exhaustion, in the process of completing the task of belonging: work.

Pleasure, experienced without requirement for pursuit, can be detrimental, creating a shallow feedback loop of empty reward and addictive pleasure from what is immediately available for consumption. In the poetry I read, the sense of belonging triggered by food is part of a mnemonic process of parsing labor, power, satisfaction, and spatiotemporal coherence. There is a kairotic physics through which the timeliness of feeling satiated provides the body an enjoyable experience that contextualizes, in a subjective narrative context, the nuance of food as a historical and economized site of work. What makes the poetry, in other words, are the lyric movements that traverse rather significant distances, whether geographical, temporal, or symbolic, and allow the body to feel settled within the inanimate objectivity of food, as an objectivity crafted by human hands and imbued with human intention. Intention matters if poetic address "constitutes" things, especially things with feelings or things with organic, pheromonal realities intersecting through vulnerabilities and expenditure.

If food is so pervasive, so necessary—so necessary that researchers find within archeological sites evidence of small fires, venison bones, and so on—and if food is *settling*, what can possibly compete with it when it comes to what a culture values? What else pervades our environments such that bodies seek belonging in other forms of feeling held, or settled? I think a more meaningful question, and one I am thinking through is: *what's the difference between anger and hate?* How can we permit anger to coexist with belonging under the democratic banner, but declare hate to be so destructive? My quick answer is work. Anger still encourages modes of labor that confront capitalism's destructive tendencies toward human well-being, while hate functions as an exceptionalist rationale toward the targeted proliferation of capitalized spectacularizations of bodies displayed in positional, precarious moments of expenditure for the enjoyment of an audience empowered by the communal tenets of white-body supremacy. Or, as Menakem explains:

> *Beneath all the exclusion and constriction of trauma, white-body supremacy offers the white body a sense of belonging.* It provides a false sense of brotherhood and sisterhood, of being part of something intrinsically valuable.
>
> A variety of organizations, from the Ku Klux Klan to the NRA, have capitalized on this, offering quasi-community, a manufactured history, respected elders, cohesive symbolism, rules of admonishment, and internally cohesive (though toxic) worldview, and so on. White-body supremacy partly soothes white bodies this way. But white-body supremacy partly triggers the historical trauma embedded in those bodies.[31]

Triggered, but also encouraged to fulfill a sense of belonging in ready-made constructs rather than seek out modes of process that involve other bodies working through retained pain, hate becomes an opioid replacement for the hormonal pathways that engage expenditure and reward within the complex narratives of subjective enjoyment. While Americaneity might be a subjective narrative that includes working through difference toward the reward of belonging understood through the flavors and smells of food, and memories of the nonsupremacist hands that cook and gift food, under white-body supremacy the joy of being American can be hormonally achieved by simply hating Others and hating any sense of responsibility toward engagement. What I'm wanting to think through is Americaneity as a context within which centuries of exposure to structural reality has created emotional environments within which affect reflects chronic exposure. Hatred toward those who feel they are victims to injustice reveals a complicated desire when it comes to justice itself. It reveals, at least to me, an anxiety over the production of justice through relationships that mitigate the survival of a justice system at specific historical moments, in that the dominant cultural belief or faith in justice as a benevolence belies the work of revision and rescripting required for justice as a plasticity. White-body supremacy is, among many performances, also an austerity in the distribution of justice, which is another way of thinking about the accumulation of "justice" signifiers. I wonder how, over time, these exposures to a self-righteous sense of dominance over definitions of justice or austere justice create ways of knowing. If we understand feeling to be a mode of knowledge constructed through the unique sentience that involves "touching" as framed by Muñoz, how do these ways of knowing inform bodies on an ethics of relation premised on what neurobiologists call long-term potentiation and long-term depression? Affect, anger, happiness, ambivalence, nihilism, joy, and so on—these are more than just dispositional descriptions. They frame modes of coautonomous exploration that may potentially resolve retention, open futurity, or recognize the hereness of bodies engaged in the project of being human.

Work and hate differ in the negotiation of trauma. In our era of archival availability, of being able to call up, cite, record, and verify witnessed events, including historical events, negotiating trauma sits somewhere between personal soothing and communal timeliness. It becomes a form of labor that takes up time otherwise valued under capitalism as a division of space, or positionalism, and the preservation of privilege as a body's immunity to somatic work. Even in my university setting, an environment wherein the kind of work assumed by the culture at large is a thoughtful one, faculty and staff reticently complete the required trauma training for our state system.[32]

While white-body supremacy has been allowed to pervade our environments in a manner that facilitates the immediate pleasure of belonging, when folks share the difficult stories of how they've come to negotiate belonging in America, there's maybe something to learn about process as a kind of soothing that opens pathways for the long-term project of not just feeling like we belong, *but building the environments we wish to belong to.*

Belonging through our pain is not to be spectacularized. It's to be understood. Soothing should/could operate as a civic principle in places where capitalism has occupied our sense of time and the partition of space between us, but soothing also asks us to consider forms of survival that take up social time and require social bonds. I remember food poems feeling like an obnoxious site of othering when I was learning to write. I refused to engage in writing on food. My one and only intentional piece of food writing came in the form of a prose piece I wrote in a class being taught by John d'Agata. I wrote about eating soup in the house I grew up in. Soup my mother had just finished making. I was a maladjusted student and carried a lot of baggage. Thinking about my home was a way of avoiding work that reflected on my upbringing and my inability to form healthy attachments in the present tense. I remember D'Agata sitting with me in his unadorned office, and we read the piece together line by line. I didn't understand what he was doing at the time. Spending such careful time on each sound as if we were treating ingredients with the care my mother's hands handled every single element of a dish that becomes soup, literally a consistency. Sitting with him hearing each line was soothing. I remember it still. I didn't appreciate that I was drawn in by the calmness and security of his body as it hummed the writing back out into the room. The essay wasn't about what I feared or worried it was about: an economy of food writing and an intrusive gaze into what hurt inside me. That one piece was about me missing something and using that pain to avoid thinking about *how*. It was about feeling an ongoing discomfort that would take another two decades to figure out. Namely, that we hurt. That we can be hurt. That it is quite common, in fact, that some of us hurt a lot.

It's not a question of *if* we experience neuromodulation plasticity in learning to survive present historical trauma through bonds and belonging that offer immediate respite versus long term contentment. It's more a question of *how*. Of what it looks like as we negotiate adaptive plasticity through collective negativity as survival. It's a question of what it looks like inside our bodies to reform attachments in a way that secures well-being, while explicitly challenging the very mechanism of autonomy in our historical envelope: nation.

It looks, I am arguing, multidimensional. It looks like a transhistorical examination of shared trauma, and the lyricization of attachments toward the demonstration of coherence: a coherent language, identification, temporal coherence, worlding. Up to now I've been focusing on negativity and somatic adaptation in poetry. But I also want to think about trauma and adaptive attachment, systemic or structural adaptiveness, aesthetic expressions of caution and community, and the (epi)genetic spatiotemporality of planning, or preparedness against the evidence of negative influence toward positive worldmaking.

trauma

Dear Diego,

This Brown body in repose is never quite in repose, always in question of who will see it, and will they be a threat—do I die today, like this?—this body full of colonization-dystrophy with its instinct to feed upon the flesh of my oppressor? How are you supposed to politely reject your suffering? Genocide is not a matter of opinion.[1]

When I read Angel Dominguez's *Desgraciado: The Collected Letters*, I am invited into a reflection of my own processes of making sense of hemispheric subjectivization. Doing so alone, I hit a block. When the archive of observable experience is burned, redacted, or banned, there is no foundation for a language to communicate experience. But it is also not entirely without bodily significance. Fire consumes oxygen. One of the scariest thoughts about burning is having your speech consumed by fire and not being able to yell out. Maybe this is why burning has played such a visible and aestheticized role in the interaction between Europeans wanting to silence the ability of Black and Brown bodies to speak in their own tongues.

When framing the situation from which language emerges rhetoricians refer to "a natural context of persons, events, objects, relations, and an exigence which strongly invites utterance."[2] Culler's definition of vatic utterance, to include here another mode of emergent language, as emanating from "a poetic speaker taking up an active relationship to a world or element of the world constructed as addressee, an addressee which is often asked to respond in some way" sounds a bit similar. What is the difference between lyric and rhetoric when you both need something, urgently, and the context of that urgency is an emergency? Culler spends a great deal of his scholarship outlining the existence of genre in relation to the actionable world, which is an important bridge to fortify. There is a lost sense of trust there, however, because "action" accounts for activities that don't unsettle cultural consensus as well as those that promote dissensus. Reanimating this trust requires engaging the poetic link, as a sensible reanimation of those "dissident" and "fugitive" voices burned into embers, as a reanimation of poetic purposefulness. Rhetoric is purposeful. Are we all of us prepared to say the same about poetry?

Poetry asks us to consider the humanity in the situations from which lyric acts emerge. To me this is a calming realization, a settling realization, because it somehow verifies that we don't face circumstances completely alone. We are always with the poetic archive. For white-body poets like Bob Hicok this heterogeneous witnessing of the world has shown to be a more unsettling realization. In his now well-circulated and responded-to essay, "The Promise of American Poetry," Hicok writes the following:

> Under-represented poets are creating a large and dynamic public space in which they can openly express who they are and be rewarded for doing so. At the same time, the public space for straight white men is growing complicated in unprecedented ways. Straight white male concerns and tropes—which have often been grounded in a context of possession and power—are being supplanted by issues that, though familiar, have never held center stage. Poetry now is more reflective of the makeup, tensions, desires, and needs of a broader swath of Americans than ever before.[3]

Even in "honest" disclosures like Hicok's there is the restating of "control" and "power" as the central tenants of public ownership and very little space given to the possibility of allyship or transformation, change, plasticity, or growth. By this I mean that instead of acknowledging that he, a white-body poet, *could also* address the political history that "under-represented" voices speak to, he instead laments the loss of sales. I'm being a little reductive maybe. But the point stands that the very realization that the public all poets address and intersect with is the very same. Those "tensions, desires, and needs" were present when Hicok was still relevant, as much as they were hundreds of years before that and continue to be relevant now. He could explore his affectively adaptive experience in the world. Instead, Hicok goes on to say:

> To the stories we've long told about democracy and opportunity, we're beginning to embrace narratives of oppression and exclusion. While these narratives have always been there, they've never been mainstream,

but as minorities become a collective majority, as women move from the background to the foreground, stories of oppression and exclusion become axiomatic and politically necessary if we're to have an engaged citizenry. Politics, in this context, is the natural territory of art. To be involved, people need to be seen for who they are, and poets are doing this. They're telling these stories and it no longer matters if straight white guys are listening. We can choose to listen, but we can no longer dictate the terms of the poetic discussion. We're part of that discussion, but we don't control where it will go. In American poetry right now, straight white guys are the least important cultural voices, as was inevitable, given how long we've made it difficult for others to have their say.[4]

The historical tide poets like Hicok refer to feels like a "wave" pushing from behind toward an inclusive marketplace and is also never characterized as an opportunity to change the public ear toward a more civic one. The marketplace is of importance above the health of its inhabitants and is never a consciousness attentive to those who are struggling to breathe. Hicok's is a performed "grievance" but not a dissensus with the very system he admits being an accepted member of, as "straight white guys" who've "made it difficult for others to have their say." Instead of offering allyship, change, participation, his grievance reinstates the valor of honorable whiteness; if it is not the seat of power, it collects what feels closest to power, like toys, and goes home. His is a mimesis of haptical reorientation, of looking for touch through feeling one's way through the sensible. But it's not the same thing, because his acceptance, by his own admission, of the de facto privileges afforded "straight white" cis-masculine bodies, never had to be accomplished through the somatic-cognitive work of fostering prosocial behaviors from the dopaminergic hapticality of fugitive *aesthesis*.

The nervous paranoia exhibited in Dominguez's epistolary speaker's "repose," on the other hand, as one that "is never quite in repose," describes to me a state of chaos I'm more familiar with. It is the chaos of being made up of experiences that are not perceptible or observable to the shared world from which the stimuli undergirding them emerge and originate.[5] Because our environments remain governed by principles of colonial exigence, and even as demographic tides shift, those who leave space for others refuse to withdraw their conceptual ownership over the emotional values that chart the coordinates of historical agency. It's the state of living in cities of ghosts, devious little troublemakers trailing legitimate figures, both historical and present, causing a mischief and pain that their corporeal others fail to see. It is living through the frustration of not having one's truth validated. Validation is the premise of a very specific kind of social agency. But validation shares genetic material with vulnerability.

> We attempt to identify the ways in which whiteness perpetuates nonwhite human suffering; this means having to untangle the system of systems from the genetic phenotype. It's important to me that my students understand how white supremacy is not simply a kind of phenotypical disposition held by white people. Much like empathy, this behavior and its toxic beliefs are learned. They are taught and reinforced. It's not something anyone is born with. I wonder if you knew of whiteness when you were still breathing, Diego. I wonder if you understand what I mean by whiteness, when you read it now?[6]

Trauma is a lived incoherence where one is taught about lack in the language deployed to disarm one's self-confidence in this world, toward facilitating exploitation. In a Bayesian[7] manner, the experiences I am actively told are not observable are therefore defined as not probable. Yet I read Dominguez's collection of letters and am struck by the resonance, the affinity. The conflation of colonial violence with governance makes for a unique sort of atmosphere to grow up inside. And I use this spatiotemporal idea, to grow up in a place, under a sky, sharing a feeling with others, because it's maybe the only way to get at the problem with feeling things about publics, shared history, and political unfoldings in America. It gets at what experience maybe is at a neurobiological, somatic level of active worldmaking, which along with cultural production and aesthetic artifacts include cognitive predictions from past experiences when those experiences in their totality are violent and traumatizing.

I say somatic here and not phenotypified. Living in a purple America, especially, enforces a code of deferential politeness to the fragile hold whitebody supremacy has on the cultural creativity bursting where people meet nowadays. This creativity is the brain and the body forging pathways into vatic temporalities and adaptively living through the traumas entire communities are enforced into believing are not probable. There is no phenotypical truth to morality, as colonialism insists in its eugenic exceptionalisms, only a somatic truth to how morality is a weaponized operation of many other canned experiences like law, education, health care, labor. Where some of us gather and how we plan, how we share and remember together, has become a forbidden site because of what might be drawn clearly from the chaotic, mnemonic storylines we bring. A hidden city from the probability of public opinion is a fugitive city, an assembly where we, among other vital experiences, verify our pain. Trauma, like genocide, "is not" in Angel Dominguez's words, "a matter of opinion."[8]

Writing in *The Cultural Politics of Emotion,* Sara Ahmed argues that "emotionality as a claim *about* a subject or a collective is clearly dependent on relations of power, which endow 'others' with meaning and value," which aligns with what I have been trying to establish.[9] But this doesn't fully address something almost epidemiological when it comes to emotion; specifically, how negative emotions policed across publics toward governing bodies according to white-body morality refuse to acknowledge barriers to public expression, even while these moral principles erect the obstacles bodies become entangled in and frustratingly call out from within. Policed into silence or suppression, disavowed expression accumulates toxically. Accumulative toxicity and accumulative ontological aesthetics intersect at the soma, and somata communicate between generations. They are both absorbent and adaptive, communicative. This is a theoretical challenge as much as it is an epidemiological one. Sylvia Wynter's historico-anthropological account of Modernity and colonialism attends to the accumulative, haptic strata Dominguez peels away with each letter.

> However, at the same time as the West initiated the process by means of which the projection of extrahuman causation could no longer be mapped, in good faith, on the physical levels of reality, it would also begin, in the wake of its reinventing of its descriptive statement as that of Man in its first form, to identify as its Imaginary extrahuman Being the figure of "Nature," now represented as the authoritative agent on earth of a God who, having created it, has now begun to recede into the distance. So that as the earlier Spirit/Flesh master code was being relegated to a secondary and increasingly privatized space, the new rational/irrational

master code, which was to be the structuring of the rearranged hierarchies of the now centralized political order of the modern state, was being projected upon another "space of Otherness."[10]

That space of "Otherness" would be organized around demonstrations of irrationality as defined by the requirements of a privatized "Spirit/Flesh master code." It is indeed an extrahuman demonstration to exist historically, yet stoically in the face of stochastic events with traumatic implication. One must ponder if it's made possible only when certain bodies are designed to be targets of traumatic experience and thus solely burdened with the neurobiological reality to react in that nexus of observable contractions we call "feelings"— as if maybe certain bodies are physically pained, or tortured publicly but in a public where the flesh and the spirit are not welcome, not observable or qualifying displays of "Man." Political "Man." This refusal becomes anticipated intergenerationally and begins to shape national and indeed transnational definitions of who gets to feel things, and what feelings are valid, making for impossible yet biologically inescapable attachments to trauma and traumatic history for many non-white bodies.

> The history of 56 million ancestors erased and executed. Enough ancestors to affect the climate of the planet. Setting fire to the master's house. I'm still locked inside the language; it is still on fire; these atrocities just won't die. I'm still burning with revenge.[11]
>
> When you set the Maya language on fire I can't help but think you had these evil aims of erasure on your mind. It was July 12, 1562, when you decided Maní Yucatán was a proper pyre place for your auto-de-fé it was then you stopped my ability to speak beautifully and, while I hear the song in the night of my heart, I don't know the words. My body is quiet. Stripped of its mother tongue, my body is compliant. My body searches for its organs in the rubble of its oppressor. My body sifts through the language patching shards together until there is an echo of the song. The mother song. The first song still sleeping in our blood. The blood of those who remain. The blood of those who remember. Remember that there was once a song that sounded nothing like these trees. Remember there was a song that sounded something like "home."
>
> Love, Angel.[12]

"I do not want to think about emotionality as a characteristic of bodies," Ahmed continues in the passage quoted above, "whether individual or collective." And I wonder: what if we do exactly that? What do we learn about bodies in our hemispheric context when we understand that some are "still burning with revenge"? What if we learn the way Dominguez's "Angel" does? Ahmed's intervention reflects "on the processes whereby 'being emotional' comes to be seen as a characteristic of some bodies and not others," which echoes Wynter's historicization of political Modernity, and premeditates the positional differentiation between political agency and what political theorists refer to as the indirect presence of non-white, morally disqualified bodies feeling something out loud about their disqualification in public forums.[13] By this Ahmed seeks to upend the eugenicist empiricism upon which colonialism establishes publics as sites of performed personhood and citizenship via affect and permissible feelings; namely, any and all feelings that underscore positive attachments to history and colonial nostalgia.

"Emotions," Ahmed goes on, "operate to *make* and *shape* bodies as forms of action, which also involve orientations toward others," and it is in this dynamic nexus that I want to place Dominguez's work and the idea that there is an immunological dilation that results from the continued exposure to the arrangements established by colonialism and carried out contemporarily. We see this in the speaker's language and pronoun repetition in relation to "burning" and public spaces, eliciting interstitial swelling and a dampening of movement. It is a blood filled to its excess with non-hematological materiality, non-cellular matter. It is, rather, comprised of historical references etched into the thick bark-ash like chicharron, sclerotic targets of colonialism and settler-occupation, coded in "songs" and "memories." The acoustics of ghosts even. There is a felt and prolonged interplay subjects exist inside of. In its best effort to articulate that feeling without a public language the body becomes an exigent site for making an impassioned case against colonial disavowal and the exclusion of those emotions from public discourse.

What becomes of environmental stress wherein enough "ancestors" have been erased through burning so as "to affect the climate of the planet"? How do our bodies adapt and respond through both interoceptive and intentional affective plasticity at this level of pervasive and ubiquitous, yet equally historical and provable violence? There is a very important line to draw between the built environment of hemispheric modernity and what we are indoctrinated to interpret purely as the stochastic events of mere existence. Mortality and event may continue to remind us that we exist spatiotemporally, but there is a difference between this sort of objectivity and spontaneity and the systematization and operationalization of the world, and the kinds of targeted violence and subjugation otherwise known as *ethnostress*.

The term "ethnostress" comes from Native accounts of the totalizing distress experienced by Native women and is used by Agnes Williams. I borrow the term here in the context of Dominguez's letters to highlight what I refer to as dilation. Spatiotemporal, mnemonic, and even affective dilation is the concurrent dislocation and organization Dominguez's letter writer navigates toward self-identification and through scrutinizing feelings of "coherence" in the lingering social attachments of colonial contact. This brings forth a chaos that is also not phenomenal, but rather gratuitously fleshed, real, and lasting. Dilation opens a mnemonic-cognitive pathway for the epistolary speaker to process hemispheric colonialism's obsession with the non-white body and the artifacts and texts Indigenous and Black bodies produce during their worldmaking. The archival repertoire passed down through informal generational channels garners textual existence in the citational practice of Dominguez's letters, a sort of melding of epistolary and docupoetic practices, while using the unique feedback technology of the epistle to recreate an acoustic-epistemic environment wherein the letter writer establishes their dualism through self-declaration, no matter how stressful.

As a mind-body awareness, dilation also encompasses the present material reality of the soul nerve as discussed earlier, from which coherence gathers alternative coordinates for self-identification not permitted in openly public or social manifestations of attachment. So, I'm not just talking about the body-to-body relationship of feeling "settled." Both Wynter and Ahmed show how the colonial tactic of alienation makes this an obstacle for many communities and their ability to pass down knowledge. But interoceptively, as a complex of nervous and hormonal signaling, Dominguez's uttered mind-body reflection through the figural audience of de Landa as a proxy of white-body exceptionalism, occupies the interstitial tissue and neurobiology that makes up that other definition of the body.

My argument here hinges on a bridge between the social body and the soma. I want to take a short detour to establish that the cognitive-somatic model I am relying on refers to growing knowledge in neuroscience that not only is the brain an active prediction-making organ (and not a passive receptor of stimuli), but predictive cognitive disposition involves more interoceptive immunological activity than we might think.[14] As we experience somatic responses to environmental stress, most observable in immunological activity that includes interstitial swelling, for instance, adaptations cascade in a manner that directly impacts neurocognitive behaviors like predictive worldmaking. I will get into what this might imply in terms of transgenerational adaptations in the last chapter. For now, I want to stress how colonialism has coopted this bridge and operationalized it completely.

When I read work like Dominguez's, I feel something akin to empathy. Some of this is due to the epistolary delivery, in that the speaker speaks for themselves, or rather writes themselves into space and time. Thus, my reading in this chapter will follow a different pattern in that I let the letters utter themselves into the space of the chapter without any direct "unpacking" as it were from me. My role is in responding to the environmental context wherein the speaker experiences the urgency to produce speech, an urgency that is met by the unequal power to make the speaker wait to be spoken to (which is not coming). It is a fervent emotional response to the continuum of violence and erasure as strategies for disqualifying how certain minds express their feelings about somatic stress in front of others.

Poetry permits passage to the migratory and haptic love of the soul nerve by decolonizing the bridge between the felt and the observable, the intimate and the empirical. The body, hardwired into the operationalism of colonialism as a world-producing/extracting system may be denied the expansive mobility to outrun the trauma of being dislocated from the world as one of its organisms. But there is a method for exorcising this occupation. This body is the site of an unending subjugation according to rules interpreted by the religiosecular madness of the colonizer. It is also a constant living somatic system of explosions and cascading reminders glowing with "one hundred megawatts of butter."

Dominguez's letter writer's queer identity further underscores the unique kind of obsession demonstrated by processes of "colonization, sexual violence, dehumanization and marginalization of who" the colonized potentially are.[15] In Wynter's analysis, the enforced cis-normative identity of "Man" articulates the demarcations of permissible love, partnership, and attachment, on one hand, and on the other, in a more traumatizing manner, designs modes of

FIGURE 5. *De Negro e India, sale Lobo. Negro 1. India 2. Lobo 3.*, c. 1780.

traumatizing bodily expenditure wherever it manifests outside those values that capitalism and morality verify as probable. It is within this framework that the epistolary nature of Dominguez's lyric project garners as much power as it holds, in terms of reflecting on publics in our "Western" world toward the constitution of poetic audience. What "is personal and intimate—whether [one's] family history, the perceptions of [oneself] as an individual, or perceptions" of one's children, particularly those in vulnerable queer and female bodies—this "becomes the centerpiece of power relations between peoples and societies."[16] While the letters exhibit anxiety and paranoia over attachment to a long-dead sixteenth-century monk, Fray Diego de Landa, the trauma-centered exercise[17] of penning such a prolific collection of letters casts a light on the true spectacle: a public bonfire in Maní, Yucatan, where texts, artifacts, and an entire embodied sense of settled security within the world are burned openly, freely, aggressively, politically. Bodies and their function between intimately functional, emotional, and physically available outwardly expressive realities are transformed into a spectacularized centerpiece of governance in the flickering movement of made light and the acoustics of this event live on in the very atmosphere.

A "body full of colonization-dystrophy," there is a pixelated space of interpellation wherein this immunological response, this survival-plasticity, produces a fuzzy aura of somatic cells and epistemological exceptionalisms braided to phenotypical casta, chattel property, and social positionalism. Some of us are made to be and are kept sick, where to be "sick" is to have the body marked and then treated in a manner over and over again until that body begins to reproduce its own symptoms of illness. This is where I locate the body of the epistolary speaker in Dominguez's work. Admittedly this prompts some important questions about the poetics, the most immediate perhaps being the question of a public in poetic theory. How are letters a public text? I think this is an important consideration, and Culler's lyric theory sheds some light on the epistolary potential of voice. But not yet. I don't want to theorize this space without reorienting the ways we sense bodies in space, because I also believe that repudiation should always first be heard and considered before its spatiotemporal location is questioned. The agency through which the letter writer addresses another brings to light a struggle over the legitimacy of governance within our cultural historical context, which relies on the dispersal of an exceptional disposition to *be* governable. This is Ahmed's claim as well. Those who are *un*governable are bodies that through subjugation are forced into a positional existence to being pained. To be ungovernable doesn't mean to exist outside, but rather authorizes the strict and violent ways of being treated *inside* a public, by the public, without cries for help being heard as just that. It is the entitlement of an audience to witness a body being traumatized so freely under a logic that decides who is gifted with feelings and emotions, as well as agency, and which bodies are simply manifestations of that which must be corrected. This public and institutionalized stress is experienced by those lives as the constant threat of permissible, even "necessary," and exigent violence. Giving empathetic intellectual space to this consideration is my intervention.

"How are you supposed to politely reject your suffering?" asks the epistolary speaker. Indeed. Poetry opens a channel to hear this repudiation as an adaptive process of rescripting attachment, I argue. And it is here that we start getting closer to the theory of publics.

∙ ∙ ∙

I've been trying to reframe negativity toward a more inclusive and active sense-making when it comes to bodies that speak up when in pain, or when cautious about the goings-on of daily life as political and historical life. These kinds of affective demonstrations are not "polite." They don't encompass polite entreaties in the sense of adhering to decorum or being mindful of fragile sensibilities regarding difficult truths about our shared histories.

> Dear Diego,
>
> ... I have to squabble with white men about who you really are—who I really am. Nobody believes me. The colonizers constantly scream at me to balance their histories and shortcomings on my head while walking a spiral of barbed wire. They scream at me to only know myself through their eyes—that dead glazed gaze of the colonizer-industrial complex. They scream at us to balance their traumas and atrocities. They scream at us to educate them and understand where they're coming from as they bleed the land and our psyches dry. They paint their faces and take back the scraps they so generously offered us by way of grants and scholarships. They scream at us to accept their freedoms. They scream until I can't hear anything but my own heartbeat and breathing. I don't have a discovery channel production budget. I'm not National Geographic. A Steller's Jay lands upon the giant sequoia outside my window. Those black eyes staring holes into mine. I know it's you.[18]

With Dominguez, and I would include transdimensional histories like those that hemispheric perspective illuminates, we begin to understand that attending to fragility has over many centuries taken precedent over attending to trauma. Fragility erupts at sites where incredulity and blaring immunological signals that action is required meet, where adhering to dominant knowledge and learned fairy tales about principles grant some bodies access to the power to decide for others what demeanor is acceptable. Caring for the coherence of dominant immunities and epidemiological stability through the exclusion and eradication of potential difference has been the priority of "place" and informs traumatizing of bodies.

I know, instinctually, what subjectivization feels like.

It feels physical.
It reaches into your cells and reshapes them like stone hands on clay.
This literal transformation is felt to be the only possible explanation.
Science tells you this is impossible. That germ cells are unalterable. But science misses the point that witnessing the sensation of these hands shaping the inside of your body exposes you to a sense that any moment might be the moment you witness another body that looks like yours simply be disintegrated, crushed into a muddy rained on dust.
It feels like an intimacy in times of public spectacularization.
While the body is a site of well-being, a site of power, it is also the vessel of expenditure most adapted to social attachment, and thus the site most apt to be exploited by systems designed to resemble attachment—but which operate as threshers of flesh. Hemisphere has taken shape around many different technologies of flesh. The encomienda system.[19] Casta like that represented. And others. And you get lost in the weird logic of having to rank which are more heinous. As Saidiya Hartman puts it:

> ... [S]uppose that the recognition of humanity held out the promise not of liberating the flesh or redeeming one's suffering but rather of intensifying it? Or what if this acknowledgement was little more than pretext for punishment, dissimulation of the violence of chattel slavery and the sanction given it by the law and the state, and an instantiation of racial hierarchy? What if the presumed endowments of man—conscience, sentiment, and reason—rather than assuring liberty or negating slavery acted to yoke slavery and freedom? Or what if the heart, the soul, and the mind were simply the inroads of discipline rather than that which confirmed the crime of slavery and proved that blacks were men and brothers....[20]

I am not talking about the body under slavery, yet. Nor is Dominguez's speaker. There is a shared epidemiological focus, however, in colonialism on the body as phenotypical expression of the world as an operation of capital, and the latter as a dominant logic of existence—a convenient narrative of the expression of the world and its contents. A logic for colonial worlding. The carrying out of settler violence simultaneous to practicing a universal juridico-moral systematization of relationships. I am talking about bodies when referring to politics. Memory. Vulnerability. Colonialism is about power, greed, terrorism, while attachment refers to an evolutionarily fundamental "tie" or relationship through which one mitigates threat and builds a sense of the future from the felt probability of survival.[21] A sense of personal history plays an important role in attachment, especially within the austere bounds of agency defined by hemispheric constitutional democracy (for the most part, though this is changing).[22] Dominguez's epistolary voice parses phenotypical imaginaries—"white men" as members of the "colonizer-industrial complex"—not out of a fetishization of difference, but because colonialism itself insisted and insists to this day on embodied, categorical differentiation as moral premises for discerning political agency.

Phenotypical casta instilled, among racialization and colorism, a language panic as well, a naming panic. De Landa's auto-de-fé equated religious and political praxis through language, and targeted Mayan codices and texts because Empire feared how its archive authenticated memory and identity outside the religio-secular order that maintained political order in its regime. Casta was a replacement, a recoding of an entire aesthetic world.[23] And by aesthetic I mean the sensible world within which knowledge was stored, valued, and communicated in all scopes of life. As I argue earlier through Mignolo, however, the decolonial project is also one of unearthing *aesthesis* from aesthetic colonialism—as the accumulated colonization of the sensible. We know now that casta paintings were the first examples of speculative artwork inspired in the Américas. They were devised as a field guide to the new territories, with the aim of systematizing phenotypical exclusion through epistemological inclusion. In other words, casta was the threshold across which bodies were dragged into a system of knowledge under which they existed as expendable tools for the building of empire.

Phenotypification and public acts of inquisition would have lasting sociopsychological ramifications on attachment.

"Who am I all these years later?" scrawls the letter writer on a handwritten page of the letters. It is the question I think all bodies should be asking themselves. The implied chaos motivates an adherence to order, no matter how toxic. It becomes a fast-tracked social survival strategy. There is another somatic relationship to the concept of chaos, however, which I've been referring to as hapticality. As Dominguez characterizes it: "I can almost feel the atoms falling off of me. Five thousand at a time. Cells regenerating every seven years while their atoms phase in and out of existence. Between realities is where I write to you. Live from the mystery itself, writing love letters to keep myself alive."[24]

If cells are actively dying off, then what are we holding onto? Germ cells, somatic cells, we've understood these puzzle pieces to be the foundation of "us," yet there is another agency that has been granted more authority than our very cellular truth when it comes to demarcating the attributes of identity. I feel the letter writer's frustration between these realities where the resetting of atoms creates an opportunity for potentiation, for change. It is plasticity, which might be love as a self-care contagious enough to spread as collective care, or politics as care. The new science in these letters is that of the hypersensitive relationship to the body in injured folk.

There is a premise of trust in the letter writer's attachment that, for this purpose, can be differently meaningful from love, itself potentially elective. Dominguez's reflections lyricized in the letters constitute the various environments where care is provided in stages of self-discovery through de Landa, as part of a family-nation structure. The epistle, being backward-looking, provides the case, which the lyric and vatic act of address animates in the present arrangements of social injustice that the poet exists through. But if it were a matter of coherence as an easily available state of belonging the work would not be "the *collected* letters." Process remains an important consideration of poetry as an accumulative and almost mycological environment of meanings and disclosures. Our neuromodulators, like dopamine and serotonin, for example, play a larger role in aesthetics than we've been truly willing to consider. If dopamine is tied to our ancestral hunter-gatherer behaviors, as the motivating hormone that has kept us alive in the cold, the barren, the necessary, and if serotonin is needed to stimulate vagal attunement, it stands to reason that throughout the last few centuries large groups of human bodies have experienced unsettling insecurity at fairly equal moments and through rather similar mechanisms of sensing arrangements and predicting outcomes. I name these colonial moments "governance" and "global speculation." Much like genocide, structural critiques of hemispheric governance are not "a matter of opinion." Governance is the *collected* documents and testimonies of those whose bodies have been transformed.

To truly and accurately describe how this feels and what it means to exist "always in question" requires upending a hard-wired logic undergirding our collective (mis)understanding about how bodies in our hemisphere have evolved to serve political, economic, and moral purposes that are intrinsic to an organization of governance that has become too deeply entangled with daily performances of identity to truly be moral, in any authentic sense. It requires not being a question, in other words, but a sentient being with voice. And so, to describe subjectivization confronts consensus realities regarding how we are collectively conditioned to feel about the political, economic, and moral exceptionalisms that frame the worldmaking faith in democratization that binds hemisphere today. "Genocide is not" and *should not* "be a matter of opinion." What is opinion? When I talk about anger, often people ask if I'm not confusing people's truths, whether I'm not, in other words, glossing over the cultural force of anger with the objectivity of truth—aren't all forms of anger evidence of different ways of truthfully experiencing the same event from different perspectives? And I think this purple-minded argument, that there is an equal permissibility to anger and hate, confuses the stochastic reality of witnessed history—what we reduce to *experience*.

I am willing to explore a neuro-historical approach to experience as a uniquely stochastic, spontaneous phenomena, because I know, also, that subjectivization maps an intentional effort to control the weather, so to speak, the "psychonormative status quo" as La Marr Jurrelle Bruce so aptly terms it.[25] Or as Christina Sharpe writes, "There is, too, a connection between the lungs and the weather: the supposedly transformative properties of breathing free air ... and the transformative properties of being *free* to breathe fresh air."[26] Reducing, or projecting experience onto stochastic, uniquely developing neurobiological individuality does not excuse the colonial design in hemispheric governance from its role in pervading violence. The randomness of experience is less random when we inform ourselves about the witnessed histories stitched across our hemispheric borders. Subjectivization, as Sharpe argues more directly regarding epidemiological reality, encompasses slavery: "exhausted" bodies and their functions. While simultaneously, as a public institution and system of permissible and violent subjugation, slavery/subjectivization was "imagined and operationalized as" the very moral and economically political system "that kept breath in and vitalized the Black body."[27] While I pick up on Black poetics in the following two sections on Albery Whitman and Douglas Kearney, I want to establish a connection to the operationalization of interoceptive and immunological adaptations to the ethnostressors communicated across environments within which Black and Brown bodies garner the material evidence of their existence and which the letter writer names between sites of sixteenth-century colonialism and present-day social politics. In the next few chapters I include trans bodies, QTPOC bodies, maternal bodies of culture and color bracing from the evidence that the fetal awareness inside them, at a nervous level, feels the world in its postapocalypse.

Proving the validity of ethnostress is the easy part. It involves how an "understanding of the strong cultural identity that existed in pre-colonial times is crucial to understanding the effects of... the loss of traditional social organization, spiritual practice and governing systems"[28] during colonialism, settler-colonialisms, and neocolonialism. Recognizing ethnostress as a targeted and intentional naming of non-white bodies implicates the legal, moral, and political instruments of governance "shifts the foundation that underlies community" itself within intentionally singled out groups, and according to various optical logics, including phenotypical hieroglyphics. Ethnostress is a rare totality, experienced by specific bodies under the gaze of the worldview that maintains it and minimizes its expansive coordination and logistics. Its existence as an affective and physically nondemocratic reality remains denied, or at minimum skeptically considered by the very same collective consciousness that centers itself as the steward of democratic benevolence and rights. Coincidentally, or not so coincidentally, this is the shared worldview that also defines beneficence as an expression of ethnonational homogeneity, a homogeneity premised not just on embodied markers, but affective performances as well.

As a component of trauma-informed methodologies considerate of Indigenous and pre-colonial worldviews, the integration of "ethnostress brought forward a way for communities to view their internal struggles," which the practitioner Renee Linklater identifies as "high rates of suicide, family breakdown, alcoholism and substance abuse." These realities challenge ethnonational homogeneity. Met with wellness processes that are both mind and body centered, naming ethnostress provides "a discussion point in which people [can] begin to explore these conditions and their causes."[29] In short, effect the formation and extension of nation as *ethnos*.

When Dominguez's letter writer ponders, "[D]o I die today, like this?" I am leveled by a concern for their well-being. They're not well, but not because of an intrinsic "illness." They're not well because they're not safe. If their predictive, forward imagining self-conceptualization is preoccupied with dying, "today, like this," they are pondering an unplanned-for threat based on evidence of past experiences that pattern their reality. They are not just *unsettled*. They exist actively in a state of de-settling and are identified through the inflicted arrangement with forces that seem to have the authority to exist publicly and legitimately in a threatening capacity.

I want to be clear about what transgenerational and multigenerational trauma is and what it is not. I am not using these terms to describe intrinsic dysfunction or illness passed down at a cellular level. "Colonial-sickness" gets described as a contagion, not a psychopathology. It is viral, taking hold of interstitial fluid and inflammation, of immunology and all the ways a body checks in on itself through body temperature, swelling, heart rate. It is environmental. It is a system and repetition. It's the "weather." Systemic exposure must shape something. The shaping principle is something sociological that replicates the same structured exposure to operationalized embodiment. The unique relationship "between lungs and the weather" keeps some folks' souls wandering, unsettled, unwell, unwelcomed home.

• • •

In *Decolonizing Trauma Work*, Linklater provides the following description of wellness. And what I would stress is that wellness is described. It is a story to tell, not a diagnosis to check.

> It was during this time that I was with my family at a powwow. My uncle and aunt had been talking about my return to the family. That evening, my uncle offered tobacco to the men sitting at a traditional drum and asked them for a song. He was given the microphone and he spoke to the people in the Anishinaabe language. He spoke about how I had gone into the system and had come home. My uncle had a very meaningful way of speaking. They brought me into the powwow circle and we danced. I could feel my mother's Spirit join us. After the song, my family stood with me as all the people came through and shook our hands. This was my sacred homecoming. It was a beautiful summer evening. The night sky was full of stars.[30]

What do Dominguez's letters to de Landa reveal when read alongside trauma-informed therapy and what are called Adult Attachment Patterns? These patterns are most commonly evaluated according to the Adult Attachment Inventory, or AAI, which lists benchmarks that function in a clinical setting to identify a person's past relational experience through the exhibition of "coherent" identity.[31] Coherence signals an individual's degree of social integration, and one should be cautious because it seems a slippery slope between social integration and expectations surrounding "healing." It stands to reason, however, that long-term potentiation and social integration are coproductive. Still, integration should not be considered purely in terms of bodies that signal positive affect despite pain or trauma. Integration refers to *adaptive* affect, which to me denotes reflexive, attentive, and informative affect: affect that productively informs the body and bodies around it of threat without retaining toxic trauma. Abolitionist work, in contrast, brings together process-centered attunement and remains expressive in a manner that permits a group to work through the existence of that threat as it stands in the public square, so to speak.

The AAI is an instrument of diagnosis, and I understand what might appear to be a contradiction between using its terms to assess a lyric speaker as a socially sentient agent and critiquing colonial epistemologies premised on categorization. I want to purposefully explore intersecting and overbearing cultural contexts with historical residues of unaddressed systemic transgressions that are at the root of personal, familial, and collective, intergenerational traumas. In that haptic messiness, bodies are meant to decipher a coherent spatiotemporal continuity within which their molecules are not being actively pulled apart, but rather regenerating a meaningful genesis for the very practice of attachment. There will always be a residual anger from this frustrating responsibility. My interest is in how poetics *resolve* the contemporaneity of colonial history and its cooptation of social bonds toward establishing embodied security without securitization. That is, being through positing experience, not Being through disavowing experiences.

Dominguez's epistolary anger is an anger at being invoked by colonial history in the present tense of neocolonial xenophobia and homophobia. At times their anger is aggressive, paranoid, resolute, contemplative and scientific, incoherent, and temporally chaotic. While the AAI is used to assess an individual's cogent awareness of self, for bodies existing in colonial-sickness, it is impossible to identify coherence without naming the "you" at the other end of their incoherence, their embodiment in historical chaos and lack, their psyche flickering like embers at the center of a bonfire made of language and silent bodies. "The idea of this book," writes Dominguez, is that "I can't quite shake the quiet of my ancestry. A lack left behind by the magic of globalism."[32]

In its authentically nonlinear examination, the letters traverse affective demonstrations of the AAI: secure/autonomous; insecure/dismissing; insecure/preoccupied; unresolved; unclassifiable. Rather than underscore coherent social integration, the letters in their whole form underline the problem of "integration" as dispositional, as policed. Thus derives the implicit and unexamined incoherence of our hemispheric cultural context as an archive that has witnessed colonialism, wherein those witnesses have been told they didn't see what they think they saw: what "lives in unaddressed violence"—ghosts. Silence. In other words, the letter writer performs these simultaneous stages toward upending the linear exceptionalism of "healing," revealing its horizon to be an operationalized invention aligned to colonial-moral decorum. How does an individual truly resolve the trauma of colonial history? What is worlding in an unclassified state of integration? This is perhaps the most fruitful question.

> Yet here I am, trying to remember what came before you, dead man. Trying to remember the color of my mother's mother's mother's mother's mother's mother's eyes. The shape of our nose. The sound of the spit that spoke non-Spanish stories into memory. What were we before all this language arrived?
> -A(nother)

Attachment presents us a window into sociality and lyric, as attachment is not premised on love or affection. Though it can. I'm thinking of the scene in the film *They Cloned Tyrone*, where Fontaine finally opens the door to his mother's room only to find a playback device on a bare desk. The molecular dystrophy of the moment collides with the repetition of his clone-identity, the unanchored memories of a life that feels authentic yet exists in no actual timeline; Fontaine enters the existential event horizon of structural erasure through structural replication of ways of being and scopes of life.

No matter how much being punished for being "godless" hurts, you can only complain so much, as the public has been conditioned to hear you only in a certain key. Understanding an individual body's processing of trauma requires understanding how systemic morality was required to deafen a community's ears to cries for help, to "NO!" yelled to the brink of exploding lungs filling rapidly with an oxygen-consuming heat. ¡CHICHARROS! From the site of Fontaine's embrace of his proxy-mother, I think about real world scenarios where attachment is coopted toward creating entire communities of bodies meant to wander through repetitive mazes, limited in what they have predictively learned they are capable of feeling or knowing about what they feel. All for the benefit of a racialized political monopoly.

FIGURE 6.

CHILDREN?

FIGURE 7.

IF YOU MEAN CAGES LIKE THIS[33]

Getting to the "body full of colonization-dystrophy" merely requires pointing to the events the letters detail through the witnessing speaker and sticking little brightly colored tabs in the archives and texts, the history those same events and their relatives reside in. Pointing out history is easy. Belief is something else. "Who will see" the body in question, and will they believe what that body has survived? What it endures? We are at an interesting moment in trauma studies, especially as it pertains to transgenerational trauma. We know that across one generation, between mother and child, there is evidence that exposure to immunological stress correlates to a strong epigenetic potential to shape heritable traits. This sort of epigenetic heritability involves a complex network of immunological signaling molecules called cytokines. Several studies have been made of these heritable, epigenetic events in children born to mothers who lived through the flu epidemic of 1918, though recent insights into the methods used reveal that the original ad hoc observation of patterns perhaps failed to fully analyze meaningful traits or data toward reaching the conclusion of epigenetic potentiation that became briefly popular in counseling transgenerational trauma. In a therapeutic context, many practitioners seek to make transgenerational connections through sites of shared trauma. This is not necessarily the same thing as epigenetic heritability, however, though it has been simplified as such. In general, neuroscience is still ambivalent about transgenerational epigenetic potentiation or plasticity over multiple generations. But what neuroscientists do agree on is that social or cultural continuity between one generation's exposure to stress or illness can very well replicate epigenetic responses in nongerm somatic cells.

Dear Diego,

The streets are full of displaced people living the post apocalypse and I am so full of rage and sorrow that it spoils into rotting pool of language. I struggle through the excess of feelings and find the approximations putrid before its petrified ... I shed the bit of you that's left in me and I pay full price for most of all my sins. Often this means years of repressed shame and guilt manifesting as mistakes and messes.... I write until you're real and disposable....[34]

• • •

Hemispheric colonialism and neocolonialism frame the cultural context and holding environments within which chronic exposure is a systematized experience, a consistent messaging between publics and bodies informing behavior, shame, and morality. The latter affective expectations for performing hemispheric personhood are part of a logic coded into categorical systems through which certain bodies are made known by politics, and tirelessly stressed by political demands on their expenditure to uphold the exceptionalist fictions of particular forms of governance under neoliberal capitalism. This is to say, *Desgraciado* is a process. A decolonial methodology making use of the materiality left behind, the archives, the remnant knowledges, the laws. "You forced death down the throats of so many," they write to "Diego," and "now I have white people to tell me about it. To tell me all about everything it is I lack."[35] As a surveyed, spectacularized body, one exudes an excess, like the physics of contagion. Our bodies exceed borders and must be contained; our emotions are excessive, songs; our tongues exceed meter and our voices are monolingual, textual logic.

Hemisphere, much like this process, is a dynamism. I use the term throughout as if I'm talking about a sclerotic, monoform represented in a block color on a map or boardgame.

Hemisphere is multidimensional, transgenerational, heterolingual.

Hemisphere exists in many of us as stories, spiritual planes, and is governed by gods and forces and powers, systems and materialities. Plasticity is the complex survival strategy wherein neural receptors create pathways toward completing repetitive tasks without expending the excess energy required when learning new movement or behavior. Hemisphere is fundamentally a human extension of our will to survive in the novel postapocalyptic arrangements inaugurated by European contact with Indigenous people, with fluidly gendered bodies that exploded the Adam/Eve worldview and desires that melted minds like butter off curves. The explicit introduction of public, authorized violence toward Black and Brown bodies in the name of moral principles and economic exigency set a motion in motion. A forwardness without history. Hemisphere is survival. Is a dictionary. An archive. A song. A memory. A taste. A touch. A fibroblast.

Epistolary poetics provide a fitting aesthetic for addressing the temporal dilation of change and cycle as they pertain to a historical moment braided to the ever-unfolding event of colonialism. There is a history of epistolary poetics in the context of "making something happen" or appear, as though making something happen were possible. The letters address how linear time moves the present further and further away from colonialism, as a history, while refusing to treat the colonial project archeologically. Keeping de Landa alive as addressee underscores the colonialism exhibited by his actions, but not as a technicality of modernity; but his violence and disregard are themselves exhibits of the very DNA of modernity. And if modernity is a euphemism for colonialism, how are we meant to re-address what has blossomed from that moment that so much political theory cites as the origin of individual sovereignty and democratized politics? Colonialism is an explicit and sanctioned methodology for the recognition of non-European bodies as global material. How are bodies, even in the beautiful sense of their capacity for art, the potential of a sculptor's hands, meant to exist truly free, given this inceptual misconception of material freedom?

The body "never quite in repose" with "an instinct to feed upon the flesh" is a body that has learned to retain a toxic memory of subjection through pain. The body learned this lesson by witnessing acts throughout history, *public acts* that equate political and moral order through the direct application of violent force. Constitutive of our political origin, public acts of violence resonate in spaces like the Border by design, and one realizes how our nation has never relinquished or deconstructed the post-colonial subject of politics, never questioned its authenticity. Resmaa Menakem points out how even the first European settlers of North America carried inside their bodies retained memories of toxic behavior conducted in the name of political morality and social order. Torture, physical mutilation, to be specific, was a fundamental tool for the systematized positionalism from which many European pilgrims were seeking respite.[36] Unexamined and unprocessed, these cultural norms on the display of violence in public, as the public, found new theatrical significance in the Americas. Demonstrating political and moral authority remained the primary objective.

What I'm thinking is this: there is indeed a creative expenditure going on that needs to be understood as the very expression of joy, as exultation, jubilation, as the kind of rejoicing that takes hold. As Elizabeth Alexander writes:

> Yes, I am saying I measure my success as a mother of black boys in part by the fact that I have sons who love to dance, who dance in community,

who dance till their powerful bodies sweat, who dance and laugh, who dance and shout. Who are able—in the midst of their studying and organizing, their fear, their rage, their protesting, their vulnerability, their missteps and triumphs, their knowledge that they must fight the hydra-headed monster of racism and racial violence that we were not able to cauterize—to find the joy and the power of communal self-expression."[37]

I am here to say that, yes, this is also happening in that void colonialism believes itself to have left in ruins and ash. But there is more to that dancing, and we need to know it lest that dancing become the entertainment center stage of more dismissive ways of thinking about how Black and Brown bodies commune with themselves. "People dance," reminds us Alexander, "to say, *I am alive and in my body. I am black alive and looking back at you.*" The misconception that spectacularization functions through is that the adaptive performance of coming to terms with the "hydra-headed monster" or with the ghosts of our colonial genes, like de Landa, somehow nullifies or pacifies any productive sense of immunological activity, like anger or inflammation, toward publicly reflecting on the pain monsters and colonial ghosts are capable of inflicting. One can very much explore healthy attachment while exploring the knowledge anger performs. It is a vital hemispheric affect not otherwise valorized by the neoliberal, democratic principles that have unfolded from colonialism's many circumstantiations of politics across the expanse of lands we call the West.[38]

De Landa's were public acts, and they live on to this day in paintings and etchings and detailed descriptions. Codices, texts, and religious objects were all burned in Mani, Yucatán. Though we might learn about the auto-de-fé in the purely religious context of conversion, the spectacular lesson of a public burning evokes a purposefully and strategically carried out act of the "corregimiento," a term synonymous with "town" or "city." Corregimiento refers to the sociocultural alignment of a subterritory to the metropole. It is the governance of a community that brands it to Empire in every moral and institutional manner conceivable. To the population under corregimiento, there is introduced a disjunctive insecurity: *what were we doing before*? Weren't we already existing? What were we doing "wrong"? What were we doing if not social, or political, already? The auto-de-fé pierces the sensible reality of an entire land with a new codex, disrupting all spatiotemporal reality. If poetry, as JS Mill describes it, is language "overheard," or voice, then are we really to believe that no one in the history of the Américas as the site of publics ever *overheard* voices crying out in pain? In protest? In opposition? Angry voices yelling: Goddam ¡chicharros! already!

Though Dominguez es un ángel, they also claim the identity of Chaac, the Mayan god of rain, depicted with a lightning bolt in one hand and possessing the power to literally transform a landscape into the ashen mud of a new form. The most beautiful of days, the most lasting of impressions from being in the midst of the estuary that is the Tijuana River Valley, for me, were those overcast days where a heavy moisture watched over us all in a gently laid weight, pressing down on us through the physics of a pulsing gray matter—the immediate experience of an atmosphere felt from below, from being bound to our humanness. I imagine those days as Chaac's.

I am being purposefully literal with Dominguez's reference to "sickness" and to "atrophy" as a way of thinking through illness as a value-laden cultural practice that moves us as a species further away from futurity even as we approach it in time. I'm being literal because chronic stress and whitebody supremacy are operative political variables with a long history of naming who gets sentient power and is thus granted a distinct kind of citizenship in the new arrangement, a history the Diné poet and artist Demian Diné Yazhí identifies as the postapocalypse. Colonialism may be thought of in relation to political modernity, but we might also consider how colonialism initiates the event of a specific kind of chronic exposure to decay, illness, and ghostliness as residency. How colonialism *is* modernity. And if modernity is often cited as the container from which the individual emerges from the ooze, so to speak, of archaic power and political display, then it is also the frame of reference for examining a very important motion as it pertains to purplish experience: from the body to the history. Dominguez makes a study of this: "Tato's mother calls it 'colonial sickness,' the latent radiation poisoning of colonization," or sees it as a "colonial atrophy," wherein one "can almost feel the atoms falling" away.[39] These are the bounds of a vatic attention to the material evidence of a trauma that has become, also, a trackable form of expenditure.

This is all rather complex. What is important is to underscore how removing sentient authority in the context of political qualifications for participation in a rigged form of governance cast a shadow on certain performances of repudiation.

"What sleeps in the violence we don't address?"[40] Ghosts. The kind of anger I'm after acknowledges the knocking mischief of America's spirits and how they possess us in degrees. The apparition of ghosts coincides with an instinctual repudiation. So, I would add that what sleeps in unaddressed violence is both a ghost and a repudiatory utterance. And maybe that's why the anger in poetry cuts people so. Why it's met with affirmation in some of us, yet another anger and refusal in others.

My faith, my belief throughout this project is that poetry gives space and language to adaptive, coherent performances and initiates a cultural plasticity through underconsidered emotional truths about who we are and what kind of environments we truly want, which are futures that can only exist as just revisions of pasts. What I'm arguing cannot be erased is how a body screams in pain or protests in anger, how that is retained somatically. What remains to be understood is whether retention and memory are enough to create changes at the germ level. What remains to be understood is how culture is to be encouraged into an empathetic moment that inspires joy from worlding, which in turn may also encourage greater felt attention to the situatedness of experience, to the considerations and contexts of justice, of law. Exceptionalism, which white-body supremacy encompasses, scripts a spatiotemporal wrinkle. Through it, the dimensionality of knowledge is the instantaneousness of denial. The possibility or impossibility of sentient intentionality behind remonstrations. Reaffirming the sentience of hemispheric bodies is a primordial consideration within decolonial analysis and study and destabilizes the moral authority of religio-secular theories of justice and the conditions of just rule.

Poetry is something. Does something. What it does is quite radical, always. Collectively, audience is sometimes enamored by its radicality. Especially and without controversy, the radicality of poetry as vatic imagination. The radicality of poetry to be "beautiful" and "truthful."

post/nation

This language is a ceremony.
The ceremony is a story.
The story is a people.
The people are alive.[1]

Poetry of negative affect advocates for expansive definitions of assembly through highlighting the ways assembly in America have taken form in transparently deconstructive and multiscalar ways, ways that have used violence as a logistic.[2] DinéYazhí's ceremonial invocation is a call to the assembly gathered together as proof of survival, existence, and generation. It is also, in its gathering, a critical demonstration of Indigenous futurity without having to choose between celebration and dismantling the genocidal desires of the postapocalypse, the term DinéYazhí uses to describe the long epoch following contact and sanctioned genocide. The cultural possibility poetry demonstrates is one that incorporates how bodies have celebrated assembly-as-survival, concurrent to histories of assembly-as-consensus to settler-colonial violence. The objective of decolonizing aesthetics to unearth *aesthesis* is especially pronounced in Indigenous poetics, and looking at both Black and Indigenous poetics better models how survival-as-resistance outlines modes of existing toward futurity within the specific limitations of our uniquely nurtured democratic nation. Thus, the decolonial project undergirding these aesthetics also upends the logic of vulnerability by recasting negative sentiment as the felt, prosocial possibilities in a radical reassembly of the demos.

Remembering that apocalypse simply means "revelation," the period of the postapocalypse is the realm of experiences with revelation and the disclosure of politics as an epoch of abusively imbalanced power and operationalized human exploitation. There is a strong historical case to be made in this period as an epoch where knowledge and discernment form a double-helix of moral judgement and white-body exceptionalism. I want to state outright that despite my focus on negativity I am and have always been interested in nation as poetics of relation. Negativity here merely highlights how relation and nation coexist in complimentary deleterious ways, the reality of each undermining the symbolism of the other, and vice versa. Even poetry that demonstrates the most radical ontological dissatisfaction with this epoch, which I would call a postnational[3] poetics, posits alternative models of assembly. Indeed, I want to argue that the utterance of postnational dispositions demonstrate acts of critical decolonization through adaptive responses to the available choices in the forms of *being* national, being American in this case. Postnational poetics reorient the grounding principles of moral decisioning simultaneous to historical revelation, and the disclosure of temporal continuums between present day nationalism and the installation of white-body supremacy in the Américas, by way of giving cognitive space and somatic representation to the sentiments of power on both sides of its application: the abusers and the abused. But, in theory, there is more to a simple binary of revolution. Postnationalism is less interested in anarchy than it is an expansive consciousness through which envisioned forms of embodied existence are not only possible but necessary for the very adaptive reality of what dwelling entails.

But that doesn't mean postnational poetics, or indeed the demonstration of postnational dispositions as radical manifestations of a love otherwise disallowed, aren't critical or don't outright repudiate the "America" that refuses to grant these modes of living the space *to* live.

In this section I turn to two historically disparate yet interconnected poets: the nineteenth-century Black poet Albery Whitman and the contemporary Diné interdisciplinary artist, poet, and performer Demian DinéYazhí. Whitman's epic *The Rape of Florida*, published at the cusp of the twentieth-century, recounts a condensed version of the Seminole Wars as a hero's tale, using the backdrop of the fugitive territories that would become Florida to chart the Edenic premise of American "settlement." But he does not consider colonial modes of existence. Assembly and liberty, rather, are experienced in the forms of dignity that runaways and displaced Indigenous people forge as prototypical personhood, or rights, within a dynamic environment of economy, relation, and affect. At the same time, the poetry foregrounds pastoral aesthetics as an anticapitalist morality aligned to principles like justice, distribution, truth, valor, and the happy pursuits of life. The tension between freedom and liberty within North American Indigenous memory situates the broken promise of modernity as an enlightened global revelation of liberalism and the social contract democratic peoples articulate in living out their time as "worthwhile." Repudiating the contradiction between value and deed, word and uttered charge, speaks to what bodies-of-color feel when in public, where the expenditure of caring is interpreted as a disqualified tax on resources like time, energy, language even. White-body supremacy exercises its own fabrication of civic or social freedom to deny love. To narrowly define love. Our dystopia is an existence where a crucial instinct of human survival, love, is erased from the record of human demonstration.

DinéYazhí engages directly with what they term the "postapocalypse." In this epoch, nation reveals itself through the unique insistence of love and carework during the emergent necessity to survive subjugation and genocide. Survival, when carried out by members of trauma-informed communities, Indigenous and fugitive communities in particular, declares constitutive desires for finding others in states of shared fugitivity as part of the survival strategies that may take shape. In doing so, in forging assembly, the bodies white-body colonialism targets for social death etch true and just definitions of liberty and freedom across the very landscapes they animate.

• • •

> Behind them were their homes, wives, children—all!
> Forth in the breach, sons, husbands, fathers stood
> To meet what came if e'en the heav'ns must fall!
> Thro' unpolluted fields by Waxe's flood,
> O'er meadows sweet and in the palmy wood,
> The armor of the foe gleamed in the sun:
> Proud was the aged maroon's incensed mood,
> As forth to meet them in a feeble run,
> He waved his servants back, and thus his speech begun...[4]

In its content, Albery Whitman's long poem *The Rape of Florida*, first published in 1882, recounts a betrayal of key American ideals played out in the forceful invasion and removal of the Seminoles from the territories of current-day Florida. Dramatizing the first two Seminole Wars (1817–18 and 1835–42) allows Whitman to disclose a long historical perspective, a roughly

FIGURE 8. Frontera, Baja, California, 2000 something.

thirty-year span, and to condense multiple historical instances of the "breach," sites and instances where the muster of American exceptionalism as witnessed by those subjugated by its logics discloses an ontological struggle played out through embodied demonstrations of defense, threat, and violence. The blatant white supremacy that deploys settler-colonial tactics in the acquisition of territory and the violent homogenization of bodies during that process of accumulation reveals fractures to the exceptionalist veneer of a singular national, liberal worldview as a juridico-centric interpretation of modernity, itself memorialized in fantasies like benevolence and singularly embodied personhood.

"Forth in the breach," provides another dimension to decolonial critique. Witnessing the hypocrisy of exceptionalism, those made vulnerable by its violence are in a position to feel the immediate indignity of being, simultaneously, put at risk of death and of being subjected politically to the role of ciphers in the various historical narratives that sustain the exceptionalist

identity of nation: of being, in other words, at risk of being made spectacle. When these witnesses speak poetically in Whitman's work their language, the poetic speech act, goes beyond direct critiques of the juridical, epistemic, and moral institutions that exceptionalist violence creates in its attempt to homogenize. Through emotional and historical reflections, these witnesses initiate a reorientation toward counter-ontologies to colonialism as episteme. These acts, moreover, introduce and animate sensory archives of events often ignored in dominant historical discourses.[5] Our coming to these sensorily rich ontological reflections signals what I refer to as a reparative historical moment and centers a mind-body principle of assembly through novel carework bridging the Black tradition and Indigenous values. The history of carework in Black communities as modes of survival in this present analysis remain "fugitive" in the American construct,[6] where fugitivity describes modes of resilience, resistance, survival, flight, and creating assembly through enacting moral values in civic actions.

Archives of witnessed emotional and historical memory find their way into aesthetics, and it is in this simultaneously aesthetic and decolonial strategy that I locate Whitman's poetics, as well as what I refer to as the poetic-political theory of his work. The latter describes how his approach to emotional and epistemic realizations, which his poetic speakers address and articulate at the sites of witnessing settler-colonial violence, returns the audience and the speakers themselves to the sensory. Whitman's speakers portray a historical-sentient orientation to "rights." Voice, between lyric and vatic consciousness as rhetorical critique of liberal logic, shifts our attention away from the dominant and exceptionalist narrative of American expansion toward a knowledge of America as a spatiotemporal reality that verifies a Black ontology of liberal democratic experience, one experienced in Black feelings, Black speech, and Black metaphysical reflection.

Whitman's focus on the Black Seminoles is a decolonial history lesson as well as a collaborative emotional and sensory song meant to "settle" the wounds of endurance, both personal and geographic. It's also an epic parsed in the meter provided in the commune of ontological worldview and nature. The "breach" is a locative membrane that swells and coalesces between safety and threat, liberty, and invasion. A metaphorical rupture that signifies, also, a creative attention to competing ideas and expansive values.[7] With "unpolluted fields," and "meadows sweet," one side of the breach is an idyllic land, a desirable land. On the other, an invading horde of murderous troops that wants it. But throughout the work Whitman reminds the reader of something elemental in the relationship that the Black Seminoles have established with the land they occupy. The land provides their freedom in the form of holding their substance. The land is a space-time for Being and is experienced in the ontic struggles over being free. For the Creek migrants and Black exiles that comprise the Black Seminoles, land and liberty experienced on the other side of a thin, even if permeable, wall to the American slavestate inspires the true liberal ideals. Their survival of indignity and genocide authenticates their moral compass regarding "right." From their side of the "breach," the Black Seminoles, and the reader, see American exceptionalism as the brutish force of power so many feel it to be.

Plebian, Savage, Sage, or lord or fiend,
Man hath of justice and of right a cause.

> Prior to all that e'er has contravened,
> Or e'en to man's existence, justice was.
> Right would be right amid the wreck of laws:
> 'Tis so, and all ordaining Nature gives
> Somewhere to live, to every child she has;
> She gives, and to her bosom each receives,
> Inducing it to love the spot whereon it lives.
>   (Whitman, Canto I, IX, 12)

In the same breath of address Whitman's poetic speaker simultaneously deconstructs the exceptionalist premise of a gifted group, civilization, class, or generation while providing, in its place, an alternative concept of law. "Prior to all that e'er has contravened, / Or e'en to man's existence, justice was," is a difficult ontological horizon for many to imagine, given the sheer temporal breadth. It is, one might argue, an impossibility.

The witnessing of invasion and the witnessing of reneged truce, these result in a kind of assembly that can be extrapolated as a sort of poetic-political theory that undermines the racial exceptionalism upon which dominant characteristics of nation, as assembly, are maintained. But the creative premise of this impossibility is what makes *The Rape of Florida* so utterly timeless. It foregrounds the Black ontological horizon in metaphysical and historical terms that America must grapple with. For Black life to "love the spot whereon it lives" requires knowing and being conscious of bondage and anti-Blackness, while also acknowledging how assembly emerges from the emotional and psychological event of witness. In other words, America's Black ontology is a knowledge of Being within the spatiotemporal history and contemporary reality of anti-Blackness as the disavowal of Black beings. It involves feeling something about what we know about our national past. This requires a precariousness, or vulnerability that exceptionalism, as a vain chauvinism, refuses to acknowledge. Recognition as a complimentary disposition to address, as speech, is a vital role we as readers are placed amidst a poetic work comprised almost entirely of a continuous speech act.

Lyric acts of witness, moreover, call forth history as events in time, given linguistic evidence, and in this attention to utterance Whitman devises a historical logic, an unfolding of democratic Dasein so to speak, which substantiates what settler-colonial ontology disavows. When we include the poetic narrator's disclosures of American institutional failure and anti-Blackness, which Whitman deploys in addressing the reader directly, with the native-Black speech acts that give voice to the witnessed events of settler-colonial violence undergirding American expansion, the thirty-year view of Floridian history swells to include earlier, later, and national forms of accumulation and dispossession. These include chattel slavery, Reconstruction-era failures to deliver on the Civil War Amendments, new forms of financial bondage, and impending twentieth-century disillusionments over housing, education, and so on. As I will repeat throughout, it isn't about how settler-colonialism expels the subject, but how it incorporates the subjected into its historical world view. It is about how subjection and subjugation, in various and practiced forms, become spatialized along a temporal record of publics.

• • •

The postnational geography of Whitman's *The Rape of Florida* is an ontological totality verifying the existence of an America, but the history of this America is comprised of criminal acts perpetrated in the name of white-body supremacy. In fact, I would argue that the postnational premises of assembly that Whitman's Black Seminoles embody in their deeds and speech continue, in this moment, to provide the spatiotemporal reality many poets, activists, educators, politicians, scholars, and scientists reiterate as the foundation of anti-exceptionalism, while the decolonial work of poetic empathy lives in what we now refer to as anti-racist consciousness.

There is something specific I'd like to draw a circle around when it comes to Whitman's poetic setting, the territory of current-day Florida, and why I use the term postnational. Poetry happens simultaneously with the happening of a national assembly. There is evidence of that Nation.

Postnationalism "indicates a movement away from a simplistic dichotomy of colonizer and colonized," argues Ellie D. Hernández.[8] The work inherent to the term "correctly labels identities and institutions that cannot be said to have just one national identity," however, so in describing a more nuanced relationship between individual and assembly, postnationalism also points to the gap created by the material effects of capitalism, which aestheticizes a parallax through which all of us living in the shared national geography do not see or experience the ontological terror of the "national identity" positioned upon the subjugated. Those who do, those who experience the disavowal of anti-Blackness or Native genocide, for instance, are charged with the task of giving evidence of the fact of their own status. This parallax view of the spatiotemporal world we share and call Nation functions in communication with the "power differential," as Lisa Lowe has pointed out.[9] The power differential outlines where ontologies meet, how they are felt, and in what ways lasting effects of power are carried over into the next generation.

The relationship between postnationalism and the speech act in Whitman is fundamental to locating his poetic work at the intersection of race and geography, of documenting the spatiotemporal reality of the Black experience in America, as American. Whitman's postnational identity induces us to "love the spot" where we live. But not without the historical work of listening to the archive of witnesses who have experienced and endured the events of its formation. Not without feeling the brunt of America's power differential. And not without repairing the psychological trauma of negating the truth of what generations of witnesses have been telling the rest of us about state-sanctioned genocide, removal, dispossession, and moral illegitimacy.

If in its content the poem depicts a betrayal and "breach" of sovereign agreement between America and the Seminole, in its demonstration *The Rape of Florida* presents an interesting impossibility regarding the political potential of the Black record, the Black archive of experienced liberal democratic modernity, of failure in the form of poetic song. It is impossible not because of an innate deficit but because any record necessitates a complimentary system of signs and signals to be understood. America is the ontological evidence that Black people exist. But American history remains a contested and manipulated narrative of how, exactly, they exist.[10] Because Blackness is not and has never been an embodied decision for Black folks to make. It is, rather, an invention through which whiteness has defined the white-body decisions to pledge allegiance to its ideologies.

"The subtle evolutions of thought must yet be expressed in song," writes Whitman in his poem's Dedicatory Address. We have to understand the archival and social justice elements at work in the high form of Whitman's Spencerian stanzas in order to fully appreciate the insistence of Black life as the insistence of an Other ontology of the world construed through settler-colonial exceptionalism. The poem's insistence as form is the insistence of the spatiotemporal reality of voice, Black and Native voice.[11] The insistence of voice demonstrates the presence of sentience in the speakers, who in their presence, their availability to witness and give speech to the "breach," demonstrate the epic progress that is the whole work: the poetic work, and the work of assembly.

> ... poetry is the language of universal sentiment. Torch of the unresting mind, she kindles in advance of all progress. Her waitings are on the threshold of the infinite, where beckoning man to listen, she interprets the leaves of immortality. Her voice is the voice of Eternity dwelling in all great souls. ... In her language there is no mistaking of that liberal thought which is the health of mind. A secret interpreter, she waits not for data, phenomena, and manifestations, but anticipates and spells the wishes of Heaven.[12]

There is a sense of moral arc in Whitman's poetic attention to "Eternity." But I also don't think "Eternity" can only mean a speculative optimism. "She waits not for data, phenomena, and manifestations"; poetry's idiomatic situatedness, the premise of its aural authenticity, is not a science, meaning a scientific kind of epistemology through which the truth of identity is to be verified (or verified in its positional status to superiority). Given the colonial history regarding epistemology, the true path for Whitman was a harmony that only music could accord. Ivy G. Wilson refers to this ambition as a sort of "sound system."[13] Though Wilson is referring to harmony, "sound system" also makes me think of more situated technologies of sound as they have evolved over time, and I think of specters of recorded sound in otherwise silenced archives, including geological and oceanic archives: ghosts, in other words, whose screams and eloquence exist in time but not in knowledge.[14] Sound systems belie the power differential with an aesthetic proposition that an audience can approach and yet still feel. "Eternity" is also an aesthetic panic that translates into an epistemic refiguration of the power differential's parallax into our spatiotemporal assemblies, a disorientation, if you will, of sensory knowledge toward repossessing what the senses have witnessed and recorded but that our historical minds told us not to authenticate. We lose the known amidst the unknown; what is felt guides us through what we have been told does not exist to feel. The sound system patches it together.

There are tensions that form alleviates: temporality, history, progress, the soul of civilization, liberalism, moral right. Whitman's ambition in aurality confronts the tension that arises in the pregnant pause prior to redemption, which could describe the unique historicity experienced in those positioned by American racialization. Whitman was born into bondage prior to the Civil War. Emancipated in his teens, Whitman had already become orphaned and had migrated between Kentucky and Ohio before settling into a prominent role at Wilberforce University. Living through Reconstruction, Whitman also became a prominent figure in the AME Church, publicly renowned as a speaker in the African American national community. In his later life he would be criticized for not espousing a militant enough attitude toward racial politics in America.

> Prior to all that e'er has contravened,
> Or e'en to man's existence, justice was.
> Right would be right amid the wreck of laws...[15]

Prior to society, prior to its record, after its assembly's dissolution, amidst the "wreck" of liberalism; no matter the form through which we come to know or experience it, Whitman argues that there is already an ethical demonstration of assembly within which we must think of performances of address and recognition. Though Whitman's conceptualization encompasses a Judeo-Christian worldview, it remains nihilistic to the structures of assembly sustained by an exceptionalist nation-state.

> If earth were freed from those who buy and sell,
> It soon were free from most, or *all* its ills;
> And
> What meant the actions of the great and good—
> The Christ and his Apostles—holy men!
> Why wandered they about in solitude,
> Despising what the world called greatness then?
> Why shun the num'rous city's places, when
> Eternal themes in their wandering tongues inspired—
> Why, but to reach Edenic sources again
> In nature?[16]

The settler-colonial desire professes to control and harness what governs itself, Nature, and indeed uses the rhetoric of the "good," borrowed from the natural, to compose metaphors for a world order based on ownership and governance. Against this construct Whitman's nihilism does away with a sense of governance as "good" ownership all together, in favor of the bodily autonomy that Nature provides, even alongside agricultural and nation-state models of assembly and material history. Time nullifies the authority of the owner. Time is the measure of freedom, not a framework for operationalizing governance.

> Thus, on a strand dividing worlds I've stood,
> Till, touched by the dark wand of mystery,
> I felt the brow of night, and earth imbued
> With dread emotions of a great eternal Good![17]

Others translate this power-powerlessness in more direct terms. Calvin Warren's "ontological terror" describes the interstice, or "strand" Whitman might have lived through in terms of an impossibility in the democratic politics of freedom to fully dismantle structures premised on the ontology, or world view, of anti-Blackness. This, we must understand, and indeed I will argue, comes to not only encompass our historical vision, but indeed serves in maintaining the spatiotemporal realities that reaffirm its many forms of norming violence as morally legitimate and legally exigent. "Freedom exists *for* Being," Warren underscores, "it enables the manifestation of Being through Dasein."[18]

Our metaphysical notions of freedom also reduce anti-Blackness to social, political, and legal understandings, and we miss the ontological function of anti-Blackness—to deny the ontological ground of "freedom" as it works to demarcate a sociality in which white-body supremacy can continue to legitimate its fantasy by severing the non/relation between Blackness and Being. What I am suggesting is that our metaphysical conceptions of freedom neglect the ontological horrors of anti-Blackness by assuming that freedom can be attained through political, social, or legal action. This is a humanist fantasy, one that masks subjection in emancipatory rhetoric.[19]

In his poetic demonstration, his poem's performativity, Whitman seeks out alternative ontological events of this metaphysical freedom, which he finds in the alternative sovereignty nourished in the Black Seminole nation. The assemblies that have witnessed and do witness the "breach" authenticate different heroes and criminals from the historical narratives curated by perpetrators of settler-colonial exceptionalisms. But Whitman also finds this in the spatiotemporal form of the very territory, as a natural scene.

Upon the shells by Carribea's wave
I've heard the anthems of the mighty sea;
Heard there the dark pines that their voices gave,
And heard a stream denote its minstrelsy—
How sweet, *all* lonely, was it there to be!
The stars were bright, the moon was up and clear;
But, when I thought of those who once were free,
And came at wonted times to worship there;
The sea's deep voice grew sad and claimed of me a tear![20]

The Caribbean as an archipelago of strands, and breaches, carries an archive of voices. Death rites, speech acts, uprisings, liberties, all "anthems of the mighty sea," all a "sound system."[21] The simultaneity of multiple assemblies reiterates the postnational claim to liberalism. This speech act ends in lamentation, in a loneliness. From that loneliness we as readers sense a call to join the speaker in the affective conclusion regarding history as it is stored in nature and its evocative scenery. It is vital that we approach the lament conscientiously, however. That we approach the "breach" for what it is, an ontic and real horizon between a reparative ontology and the violent ontology that maintains the ontic trauma, or anti-Blackness. The purpose in approaching the "breach" is not to maintain our gaze on it or fetishize lamentation, or to "keep" Black ontology at a media distance in the parallax. The act of recognition requires a restoration of an ontology, a space-time within which what is happening to us happens to us. Black ontology is the reparative ontology to the damage of anti-Blackness.

The experiences of settler-colonialism, which includes tightly braided methodologies for carrying out anti-Blackness[22] by those whose assembly and ontologies are breached, are also being recorded, and thus written. They are given aesthetic dimension, affective register, put into genre, invented upon, and archived, passed down, and so on. Their record of events travels with them when they are displaced, are shared with others in exile, are retold in the carceral nightmares that surround them and others who are similarly divorced from the liberal ontologies under which assembled life in the Americas has produced positional subjectivity. "Forth in the breach," we not only find the speaker addressing us directly, but also the poetic heroes who are mid-rehearsal of these "anthems."

Whitman locates the creators of a democratically sovereign identity. And it is one based on acts of interlocution between individuals recognized for their difference, not homogenized into a singular narrative, not on the racial fiction of purity, superiority, or an exceptionalist supremacy devised for the purposes of property monopoly.

> The poorest [B]lack that came upon their shore,
> To them was brother—their own flesh and blood,—
> They fought his wretched manhood to restore,—
> They sound his hidings in the swampy wood,
> And brought him forth—in arms before him stood,—
> The citizens of God and sovran earth,—
> They shot straight forward looks with flame imbued,
> Till in him manhood sprang, a noble birth,
> And warrior-armed he rose tall that manhood's worth.[23]

There is a strong sense of solidarity from this witnessing: "The poorest [B]lack that came upon their shore, / To them was brother—their own flesh and blood." Ethnic and racial heterogeneity is not only a marker of assembly, but moreover there is a strong theoretical claim made on liberal politics when difference, not homogeneity, is the premise for citizenship.

In a poetic twist of focus and historical consciousness, the Native and Black interlocutors of the poem demonstrate the very Americaneity that dominant American narratives of displacement, slavery, and violence seek to erase, or de-authenticate. This spatiotemporal rewriting of the historical subject's emergence from a liberal democratic "place" via Whitman's geographic lyricization of Florida, and through the various demonstrations of Black Native speech acts, reveal the very legitimacy of an American moral ground as a falsified ontology, one aligned to settler-colonial violence and the forceful white supremacist ideology that had evolved, in Whitman's own time, into Jim Crow, Black Codes, policing born out of the fugitive slave law, convict leasing, the privatization of carceral logistics, and on and on. In the heroic characteristics attributed to Atlassa, the virtue and courage given Palmecho, and the service and sacrifice of Abraham, a sovereign runaway, Whitman crafts an epic story of freedom as the longevity of an identity forged and "self-restrained" in the face of outright and authentic criminality. Whitman seems almost to say: the despotism American historical narratives position as the rhetorical situation of democratism, as the speech act of liberalism (the establishing and promoting of rights via discourse and debate), as in practice not the Revolutionary antagonist, or Empire, nor the establishment of Nation as *the* revolutionary act against despotism, but as its own genocidal disorder, in its own crimes perpetrated under cover of lawfulness, morality, and exceptionalism.

• • •

> If e'er the muse of history sits to write,
> And Florida appear upon her page,
> This nation's crimes will blush the noonday light,
> And ******'s name will lead her criminal age![24]

"Extermination was his highest creed," declares Whitman's poetic speaker of Zachary Taylor specifically, "Bondage the *one* provision of his will."[25] Absence through genocide, or slavery as social death—these are the coordinates of non-Being. "I never was a slave—a robber took / My substance—what of that?" is the poetic speaker's response to this ontology.[26] This is what I refer to as Whitman's demonstrative speech act. They identify the ontological terror of settler-colonial violence, while confronting the social death of settler-colonial subjugation, remembering that the real terror of this ontological "breach" is not in how the subject is cast out of Nation, but rather in how the subjugated are included in national history and memory. Speakers address each other, address an audience, and address history itself throughout the epic. In each instance the speaker is verifying and documenting what is witnessed, but also what is felt about the event itself.

Black ontology situates itself on the other side of the "breach," which might lead one to believe that the settler-colonial worldview, and indeed the ontology it posits, are of equal legitimacy, that it's merely a matter of circumstance and choice which ontological horizon one chooses. This is not the case. Power is at stake, and power needs to be delinked from the settler-colonial worldview its ontology organizes and maintains.

In the latter decades of the nineteenth century and following the Civil War Amendments and the reshaping of voting rights, in particular, the "extermination" and the ethical question of "substance" disavowed are contextualized in a new rhetorical impossibility, which I explore through the idea of *stasis*. Even during the liberal periods of progress anti-Blackness has manifested in violent and murderous forms, however, particularly in relation and response to juridical evolution and civic de-colonization.

I was in bondage,—*I never was a slave*,—the infamous laws of a savage despotism took my substance—what of that?[27]

Power is at stake, and power needs to be delinked from the settler-colonial worldview its ontology organizes and maintains.

• • •

Whitman is writing at a critical period of the nineteenth century, though even during the liberal periods of progress anti-Blackness has manifested in violent and murderous forms, particularly in relation and as a response to juridical evolution and civic de-colonization. I'm building toward a contemporary emergency along a historical tract that has recently, 2017 through 2020, been made visible, audible, material, and otherwise real for many outside the communities of direct, sensory witness. The unique role of governance in crafting, amplifying, and manipulating history has disrupted normed beliefs in history, itself, to a point of dramatizing governance as property that has belonged to an "exceptional" group. It is not property readily shared, or truly deemed public. The shared anger at exceptionalism-as-executive execution, or tyranny, however, is not a novel response to colonial terrorism.

It has been discovered that during the 2016 presidential election big data was used to intimidate African American voters in Floridian counties along the I-95 corridor. Whether or not it can be proven that these "deterrents" worked to isolate and mobilize (or dissuade) voters and turn them away from voting during that election, what is important is how data was used to include African Americans in a national construct and the exercise of this right, a property of the individual to vote. Again, of the lasting modes of violence through which settler-colonialism consolidated power is not how subjects were cast out of the nation, but rather how the subjected were made part of the nation, and how those institutionalized practices have evolved into sentimental permissibility and bodily interrogation. The use of demographic data in this way—counting bodies so as to dispossess subjects—falls within a problematic continuum that Whitman himself spoke against in the 1880s, including how African American voters might either be manipulated by politicians who cite freedom in attracting their vote, or how politicians and government

From: Proud Boys <info@officialproudboys.com>
Date: October 20, 2020 at 944:59 AM CDT
To: ▇▇▇▇▇▇▇▇▇▇▇▇▇▇
Subject: Vote for Trump or else!

▇▇▇▇▇▇▇▇▇▇▇ We are in possession of all your information (email, address, telephone. . . everything). You are currently registered as a Democrat and we know this because we have gained access into the entire voting infrastructure. You will vote for Trump on Election Day or we will come after you. Change your party affiliation to Republican to let us know you received our message and will comply. We will know which candidate you voted for. I would take this seriously if I were you.

FIGURE 9. Proud Boys email to Democratic voters, 2020.

clerks might purposefully violate access to voting as a way of disenfranchising Black voters all together.[28] It is part of how African Americans become included in the national ontology of liberalism following the Civil War.

warning: EFFIGY[29]

In the early 1880s Florida census data was being used to weaponize districting and representation, intimidation and dispossession, against Black voices. Its "Black Belt," comprised of nine northern counties, posed an electoral opportunity to deliver on the very promises of Emancipation. For many white Floridians, the population of Black voters in these counties was considered a threat to the ontological order that white supremacy and settler-colonialism had long established. While in *The Rape of Florida* Whitman spends ample poetic space describing a rich landscape already prepared for farming and residence as a manner of mapping the desire of American occupation, at the end of the nineteenth century it is the political possibility of the vote and representation that motivates new mechanisms of displacement, voting restrictions, carceral enterprise, and the Black Codes.

In a letter to the editor of the *Weekly Floridian,* dated July 4, 1882, one James T. Magbee of Tampa writes in the hope of inducing farmers to move to Florida: "One great advantage the farmer has here is that he need never fail to raise a crop; for if one thing fails he can raise others, as he can plant a

FIGURE 10. Effigy strung up by the Ku Klux Klan in Miami, Florida. L1986030_01, Stetson Kennedy Papers, L1979-37, Southern Labor Archives. Special Collections and Archives, Georgia State University, Atlanta.

marketable crop the year round. He need never be idle and will always find the soil returning a rich reward for his labor." There are three threads I would like to pull at here: first, the imaginary of Florida, an anachronistic and romanticized portrayal of a fecund and untouched land full of simultaneously untapped yet underwritten "reward"; second, a new demographic that emerges from the destabilizations in post–Civil War agriculture, in terms of itinerant white farmers, migration, and land; and third, an exigent fear of the Black vote in Florida's northern counties, where Black men outnumbered white voters in drastic proportion.

In terms of the first thread this kind of rhetoric exists in a hemispheric continuum of colonization that involves dispossessing others' ownership and accumulating resources.[30] Recent forms of terrorism like threatening emails sent to Democratic voters in Florida weaponize the same passive forms of abuse as previous examples of violent white supremacy, like hanging effigies of Black voters in Miami, Florida, in the 1940s.

Regarding the second, the exploitation of poor whites, including communities that align themselves with whiteness, is a long-practiced strategy for maintaining capitalism through social vocationalism. The third strategy alluded to is more revealing in relation to the 2016 tactics.

In the same issue of the *Weekly Floridian*, in its coverage of an impending Democratic mass meeting to be held July 8, the editors illuminated their readers on the situation in the Black Belt, a portion of the state made up of the nine counties: Alachua, Duval, Gadsden, Jackson, Jefferson, Leon, Madison, Marion, and Nassau. In the 1880 census the population of Florida numbered 269,493. According to the *Weekly Floridian*, 133,798 were living in those nine counties. Of that number, 90,132 were Black Floridians and 43,563 were white. In the rest of the state, roughly 37,000 were Black and almost 98,000 white. "It is in the [B]lack belt," affirms the editorial piece, "that strength of the Radical party is to be found," the "Radical party" being the Republican party at that time. "Their possession of the election machinery," it continues, "gave them opportunities for swelling their vote at pleasure and furnished the means for perpetuating their power." Much of the rhetoric used in illustrating electoral politics hasn't changed, including the reduction of voting behaviors and intentions to the mechanistic function of parts in a system, or the sum of ciphers, in other words, the transliteration of human voice and ideas, desires, and representative acts into logistics and the accounting of population, rather than its consideration.

Then comes this:

> To sum up: the "[B]lack belt" contains within a fraction of one-half the population of the State, has nearly 45 per cent. of all the taxable resources, pays about the same per cent. of all the taxes, and gives in the neighborhood of 38 percent. of the Democratic vote cast in the whole State. Its drawbacks are the presence of nearly 75 percent. of all the negroes within the commonwealth, which deprives the tax-paying people in the belt, except in exceptional cases, of any voice in shaping legislation or in controlling questions vital to the whole State and especially so of themselves.[31]

Driving home the point in terms of liberal "progress" and debate, in other words citing America's democratic ontology,[32] the editorial makes its call to the settler-colonial strategy of forming an "invading horde" and approaches the vote as it would the "breach."

Being thus powerless, the people of these counties have necessarily to look for protection against vicious legislation to their brethren of the white counties.

Just like that, 90,132 bodies counted in the 1880 census are erased from humanity, from being considered "people," and rhetorically situated as "legislation," as merely politics. But more than this, what strikes me is how the editorial invokes power in feeling "powerless," which transforms justified Black anger into a generalized energy desiring to threaten, in a reverse-racialized way, white bodies and white-body property. Blackness is literally here treated as a form of indirect power, not as the identity of sovereign persons within a nation of rights. Blackness, in other words, a specific idiom of Blackness, I should add, is revealed to be an invention that metabolizes truly affective histories, creating self-serving fictions in the place of knowing the reasons for affective demonstration. As such the invention is a fabrication within the fabrication of the ontology that establishes rule of law in relation to it, as a power against which governance must direct *its* power—the will of the people, no matter how fictional. Invoking Blackness this way as anti-Blackness calls out to white supremacy and situates images like the effigy of a Black Florida voter. The image resonates with sensory trauma and sensory language. I think about the "sound systems" of people gathered, a literal sound system of vibrating chords to cochlea, the feeling in children of their caregivers' chests rising and falling quickly as they speak, their hands becoming warm and sweat covered from the adrenaline as they remember.

• • •

Postnational poetics demonstrate the valance of human dignity within the impossible arrangement of rights. Witnessing the "breach" of human dignity is a contemporary measure of the spatiotemporal experience in America, and for many whose national identity is transformed into a fear, made into targets.

> Thus, San Augustine's church and prison joined,
> Fitly portrayed crimes' eminent success;
> When hounds and murderous troops were loosed to find
> The unsuspecting exile, and to press
> The wretched Seminole from his recess
> In hommock far, or by the dark bayou:
> To burn his corn-fields in the wilderness,
> And drag the helpless child and mother, thro
> Infested swamps to die in chains as felons do.[33]

Black Seminole dispossession played a central role in Florida's ratification, as did America's anti-Blackness in building consensus among divided delegates.[34] Statehood would come to encompass not only land acquired through numerous contractual breaches, but also through the legislative monopoly over the narrative authenticity of its constitutional history and the state's carceral relationship to Black denizens in the history of Black exiles, runaways from southern plantations and therefore "criminals" prior to Emancipation.

> "I regret to hear of the recent murders committed near Fort Lauderdale," writes Zachary Taylor to Thomas Jesup in 1838.
> & am satisfied you have fixed the real perpetrators, the Seminoles, which shows conclusively that no reliance can be placed on their promises or engagements, could the perpetrators of the act be gotten hold of, they ought to be put to death in some way as a terror to others of their nation.[35]

Two years prior, in addressing the second Congress of 1836, Jesup argued before legislatures that "This," referring to the Seminole wars, and the Black Seminoles in particular, "is a negro, not an Indian war; and if it be not speedily put down, the south will feel the effects of it on their slave population before the end of next season."

This sort of anti-Blackness survives in how the Black Seminoles were cast in public opinion, and I think of it in the rhetorical terms Amber Kelsie outlines when arguing how

> [p]olite discussions that acknowledge racial terror only so as to explain away racial violence as the unique domain of extremists maintain a sense of white innocence that not only individuates a structural condition, but also pathologizes and prohibits [B]lack utterance (especially when that utterance might take on the form of rage) by adjusting the impossible demands of [B]lackness back to the acceptable terms of debate.[36]

"Raciality," she continues, "is intrinsic to modernity because it is necessary for the construction of the Subject—it names the materialization of the spatiotemporal forms that make the modern grammar." The grammar of liberalism, Kelsie establishes, is *stasis*, civic equilibrium via debate. But Blackness presents itself as an impossibility. It is an invention evoked in certain manifestations of an ungovernable power that must be extinguished by law; Blackness describes criminality; Blackness is an influence; Blackness is readily made effigy. Black life does not matter, and yet Blackness is the only thing that matters to law and order, and to the progress of the liberal democratic nation state as it exists and operates ontologically as what is "good."

The contradiction of the American Democratic context is that, as a rhetorical exhibition of progress via debate and thus an archive of speech acts meant to overcome institutional challenges, it can only premise the human liberal project, a consciousness capable of envisioning a historical continuum of *stasis*, while maintaining, often through some understanding of violence, a complete disavowal of Black life as part of that *stasis*, of that civic equilibrium maintained by continuous speech. What I wish to highlight here is the spatiotemporal role in maintaining, perhaps not civic *stasis*, but a collective aesthetic imagination of a "place" wherein civic *stasis* needs to be, somehow, repaired and restored.

The premise of debate, itself a speech act, illustrates the inescapable and impossible ontological breach Whitman directly confronts when he writes in the Dedicatory Address, "I was in bondage—*I never was a slave;*—the infamous laws of a savage despotism took my substance—what of that?" This same ontological challenge would be posed nearly one hundred years later, in 1963, on broadcast television, by James Baldwin.

> What white people have to do, is they have to find out in their own hearts why it was necessary to have ******* in the first place, because I'm not a ******, I'm a man, but if you think I'm a ******, it means you need it.[37]

• • •

We are permanent beings. We abide to a lifeline.[38]

Indigenous aesthetics reminds us that before capitalism creation was the totality of logic encompassing time, embodiment, death, threat, survival, generations, ceremony. Part of what I have been working through is epochal. I've been referring to it as a time dilation because our mediated awareness situates us in a continuum of information that is, simultaneously, a contagion of negativity apprehending our affective, somatic selves in a way that restricts the capacity of civility to operate where instinct perhaps was, a long time ago, good enough to keep us "alive." We find now, moreover, that civility as the observable conduct from subperceptible beliefs in fact organizes ways of dying—makes those ways of dying part of a larger more permissible, even desirable, historical system. That is, makes them into what is called necropolitics.[39] I have been thinking through the kind of anger one feels when on the receiving end of permissible disavowal, of civic and democratic subjugation. This anger is aesthetic in the sense of being demonstrative through affective registers, which can be archived and traced to archives, which are informed and can be informative, which are sentient and evidence of sentience.

I first encountered Demian DinéYazhí's work through a performance titled "An Infected Sunset." In this piece, DinéYazhí reads from the work while behind them, saturating the glass façade of the Whitney, the sun sets over the Hudson, over New Jersey, over the West. The audience is brought into a space of discernment. Or rather, it is guided into the allowance of discernment as the occupation of a realm of relation. In the presence of poetic voice and a string instrument there is an attunement to the dilation of the sunset as the perceptible event of creation, as the urgency of geological time in the face of operationalized time. The offering is kairotic, is on-time, in the sense of the poem and the writing that produces it as performative, in terms of a sympathetic nervous settling and communal survival. As Diné Yazhí describes it, the work was "conceived in 2016 in the wake of the Orlando nightclub shooting, police killings of unarmed Black men, and in the midst of the Standing Rock #NoDAPL Resistance," and "the sudden revival of extreme white supremacist nationalism."[40] The shared fugitivity of these communities, which is to say, their vulnerability against civic narratives of governed behavior and "getting along," is a realm of relation bound by the affective contagion of ethnostressful stimuli. These are time-stamped in the very names the historical events spell out in how they produce a *charge* in us: a pre-accelerated significance to meaning. These are tragedies linked through the necropolitical operationalization of bodily vulnerability and a dominant desire to erase difference in all forms of rationality.

By whom? For whom?

Emotion is about checking in. Emotion is a pathway to orientation, adaptive intimacy. Maladaptive intimacy, either from internalized and retained distress or from the violence of blowing through another body's intimate autonomy for the sake of exploitation, is how colonialism has worked to keep bodies subjugated. This is how colonialism has kept bodies organized in a chain of production, away from creation. And yet, "This is not a story of dislocation" writes Diné Yazhí, highlighting an important possibility in locative intimacy, in the animation of fugitive affects as demarcating space and the ceremony of time.

Members of this fugitivity, however, when surviving, feel "splintered—shattered by sadness, shock, and fear." This cannot be stressed enough: the purpose is not the spectacle of affect but the transformative, somatic experience of being with the discomfort of affective repudiations of normative civic, white-body life. The artist and writer micha cárdenas describes the discernment required "from news of events that come in an irregular, but inexorable, rhythm," and how a performative apocalypse (revelation), including writing, "is an effort to bring" the "rhythm" of disclosure "to life and to reflect upon its significance by considering the relationship between visibility and affect and how the digital acts as a medium for flows between, through, and across both."[41] Indigenous aesthetics might seem like an odd place to introduce digital time and dimension, but it's also worth considering the digital as an incarnation of the most diametrically oppositional form of capital, as a logic, to creation. That is not to say that Indigenous creatives operate outside digital possibility. On the contrary, contextualizing ways-of-making, or poiesis, through an attention to the ways of subjugation that erect archives and platforms is responsive to both technique and technology. The adaptive aesthetics Indigenous artists have operated through are celebratory as much as they are illuminating, especially when they continue "traditional" forms of artistic making and material production while integrating intersectional desires into them, thereby transforming the cultural identities in situated language. Or as Blas and cárdenas argue: " . . . the drives and assumptions of a heterosexual sexuality produce certain ways of producing and knowing that can be embodied in objects created by heterosexual scientists, whether they are conscious of this or not. Similarly, homosexual desires can inform and help to materially construct the technicity of objects."[42]

The observable is coproduced in the availability of touching screens that bring the world up to our eyes in bits and by/ites: selective, improvisational, invited, invasive. These are stimuli that threaten the nervous peace of feeling like you are surviving, thriving, or subjugating, and they are simultaneously channels of fugitive planning. Moreover, the 2014 "emotional contagion" experiment wherein Facebook manipulated feeds affecting more than 650,000 users to see how emotions can be governed reveals how our feelings are biological realities corporations deem they own, part of a eugenics of disposition. DinéYazhí refers to the time dilation within which the threat of colonial contact measures existence as the postapocalypse. The end that has long been unfolding since the usurpation of creation as a treaty between an assembly and the landscape over which an assembly counsels and lives.

> I imagine a post-apocalyptic landscape. I imagine a blinding flash coming from the south. I imagine the line between traditional ways of living and the alien culture that is forcing their ways of living onto the people.
> The image is a reminder. It serves as documentation of a post-

apocalyptic narrative that has been unraveling on the north American continent since european invasion. Just as the image of my mother and her newborn son is a reminder. It serves as documentation of survival in a postapocalyptic narrative that has been unraveling since Tséyi' was assaulted by the united states of america's army and the Diné were forcibly displaced to Hwéeldi.[43]

That "blinding flash" is the atomic bomb first being introduced to the world in a ceremony of light and energy. It usurps the sun. It usurps the release of energy the sun culls from cells. It is the bulb flash of the camera, freezing Indigenous bodies in fictional poses, reducing life to the archive and forever keeping Indigenous bodies in the past. But it is also the bulb in DinéYazhí's hand capturing fugitive stories. It is the light released into the cellulose and polyethylene pressed into albums that tell stories bodies have been telling for generations. Accompanying the chapbook version of "An Infected Sunset" is what the author calls the "Liberated Poem," an "offering to Indigenous communities and landscapes striving for a decolonial and sovereign future emancipated from white supremacist capitalist heteropatriarchical settler colonial trauma drama." Drama here elicits the visual focus of information, as well as its potential for archival distortion and sharing. The work is a collection of loose broadsides. These attentive modes of text-making are reflected in the work *Ancestral Memory*. Between their texts and their aesthetic work, where anger and celebration meet, we are most likely to find survival as a kind of resistance to violent normalization. We are likely to find bodies performing survival in an aesthetic demonstration of expenditure, megawatts strong in the burning of butter; to see bodies enduring, desiring, knowing, and sharing knowledge through the informal archives that define generation. They are *generative*, not nostalgic or reincarnations of historical death in necropolitical connections. As a looking back to inform the present, decolonial expenditure is life-giving, affect-affirming sentience.

> Sometimes I'm not trying to decolonize shit!
> but then I remember the way love rolls thick around
> an indigenous body
> when I talk about this continent / I'm talking about a brown body /
> when I'm talking about genocide or romanticizing history /
> I'm talking about a white body /

> I can't help it / it's been engrained into me like a branding / was
> the world I was born into / was the cause of headaches and starvation
> sexual appetite and no satisfaction / shame / trauma /
> insatiable hunger / teeth gripping human skin /
> the evolution of the crucifixion of christ /[44]

The "love" that "rolls thick" is a transversal affection "around / an indigenous body," which is the recognition of embodied truth by the physical logic of viscosity in gravitational space. The liberatory sensemaking in this arrangement of movement, affect, soma, and value is, equally, attuned to the dissatisfying observability of other events: continent, Brownness, genocide, whiteness. How are we supposed to negotiate this labor? That is what fragility concerns itself with communicating in the place of participating.

We are equipped to understand how. Discernment is a radical performance in that it animates sentience as the public performance of observability. Discernment is the powerful allowance and permissibility that is part of ceremony.

> This language is a ceremony.
> The ceremony is a story.
> The story is a people.
> The people are alive.[45]

The origins of Judeo-Christian discernment can be traced as far back as the third and fourth centuries, but it is accepted that Saint Ignatius's sixteenth-century spiritual exercises solidified discernment in the world at a time when the "the world" itself suddenly manifested itself to "the people" as a sphere. In the sphere, the sense that there was nowhere else must have been a powerful feeling to negotiate: That there were no other "people" negotiating the evolutionary awareness of survival and generation. That there was a return, geographically measured against the spiritual concept of mortality, which would be understood then and after as a very specific kind of eternity, like a gated community in a southern California suburb. That one could shoot forth like an arrow and, unhindered by physics, complete the journey where the journey began, without having changed or been impacted by the dimensions pulled together by the dilation of time and movement. That is to say, the individual with the power of discernment as an awareness gifted by their own eurocentrism would be imbued also with the godly power to divide the globe into categories of good or bad spirits, good or bad influences, godly and ungodly inhabitants. This validation was the seizure of "good" and "bad" as values expressed in the world, not as the phenomena of "event" but as part of a design, part of an ongoing "war" between spiritual realms outlined in the testaments. I wonder if this naïve vision contributed to the solipsism of colonial consciousness.

Once introduced, solipsism is a tough habit to break. It finds its way into our convenience. Our toys. Our performance capitalism.

Spiritual discernment is the generative, heroic logic of an eternal exception in our hemisphere, one that has granted a state of exception through the application of parajuridical, parastatal violence.

Yet, "The people are alive."

How is this explained, given the colonial imperative to maintain the balance through violence, the economic and moral balance through displacement and enforcing the "hell" of social death, subjugation, and structural disenfranchisement? The answer is of course that colonialism is a breach of an original logic, a logic from which capitalism is crafted. It's a breach of a treaty or contract regarding primacy and focus. Creation, not Genesis. Black Seminole fugitivity. Creation as emergence, and emergence as the event for discernment in the species life of humanization on earth.

In the postapocalypse, we are in the midst of experiencing creation's emergency. Creation is urge, as in the urge to survive by discerning safety, calories, kin. Yet, in the postapocalypse we are urgently scrambling to rebalance a world out of balance. A world knocked off its axis from the internal operations of solipsistic arrows shooting off into their eager directions, causing havoc, blowing through each other, focused only on their individual survival. Is anger anything but the urgency to live in a manner other than colonialism? Is the urgency to do so as a matter of collective survival somehow not a valid rationale in this world, and not the urgency to produce, but the urgency to acknowledge the observable facts of our world that have long gone disavowed?

DinéYazhí presents a ceremonial way of anger when it comes to negotiating questions with obvious answers, which have been buried in genocide and genocidal naming. My "Mother was born into a concept of poverty,"[46] they write, which resounds with Whitman's reminder: "I was in bondage,— *I never was a slave.*"[47] "We have a white way of being angry," writes DinéYazhí.[48]

FIGURE 11. Demian DinéYazhí', trust fall (pine ridge), 2012.
Image courtesy of the artist, Demian DinéYazhí' © 2012.

What is white anger? Rage? The divorcing of emotion from creation forces its expression onto bodies, not phenomena, not survival. Survival is displaced from creation and made the subject of social death and genocide. It becomes a defensive bracing against human operationalization, not worlding. White rage meets another complicated declaration of poetic voice in Whitman, where the speaker declares that "Nature," through its extension into the world in perceptible acts, induces one to "love the spot whereon it lives."[49]

DinéYazhí's body in the photograph "trust fall (pine ridge)" faces america as it calls upon the spirits at Wounded Knee. Those awaiting justice and ceremony. Those still surviving colonialism in its contemporary institutions. This anger is about relation. About love.

I emerged from the landscape. This is my creation.[50]

¡vecinos!

FIGURE 12. Vecindario, Nestor, California, 1986–2024.

"A meteor has more rights than my people" points out Posdnous of De La Soul.[1] I think about this when I enter the intentional emotional space of writing about embodiment and bodies. I think about that when I refer to detention centers and cages, to depression and anxiety. When I write about my dad eating butter, my baby-self being carried through space in my mother's arms. When I think of the throbbing cubital tunnel pain in my mother's arms while she carries two babies through space. It's somber. It's love. It's anger. It's education.

When a meteor lands on earth it is instantly granted terrestrial rights extensively outlined by the Antiquities Act of 1906, the Federal Land Policy and Management Act of 1976 and its amendments, and by regulations established and enforced by the Bureau of Land Management, 43 CFR 8365.1-5 (1). Admittedly, a meteor isn't just any old thing. It's a pretty wonderful thing. A thing worth noting, its presence on earth worth considering. Some would argue that so is life. There are many precedents regarding the treatment of life in America also. Not all of them as benign as the rules outlining how to handle meteors. Since the so-termed founding of North America as a terrain of Reason, early influencers of conduct and code like Cotton Mather have instilled an intentional exceptionalism to reason as a code of governance through which life is lived to an exactness of Law.

> First. The Man who does not *Hearken to Reason* does Rebel against the Glorious GOD, who has placed Man under the Guidance of *Reason*. ... We never *Transgress* any *Law of Reason* but we do at the same time *Transgress* the *Law of GOD*. Now, there is always a *Sin*, the blackest thing in the World! in such a *Transgression*. GOD sets up *Reason* in Man. If we do not keep *Reason* in the *Throne*, we do *Dethrone* the Infinite GOD Himself. The voice of *Reason* is the *Voice of GOD*. ... [2]

Life, forms of it, are coded with social annotations that can be traced through legal precedents, court briefs, and moral lectures where ideas of subjugation are articulated in practices of subjection as practices of adherence to Reason. I am talking about laws and policy, a long list too comprehensive and deeply historical in the origins of social behavior as an exhibition of white-body supremacy. One should note that Reason, for Mather, and in the minds and practices of his audience, includes the reasonable sale of "willing" slaves, passive bodies in need of ownership. Of those bodies in need of conversion, the rationale of slavery was a sort of white-body charity under the Law of God. While enslaving was a transgression, purchasing slaves was not. While owning slaves was reasonable, not converting them was transgressive. Lives come to accrue textual weight in these complicated and contradictory lines of reasoning. Graphic weight. Through the history of being "stamped," as Ibram X. Kendi notes, this embodied relationship to something graspable, like conduct, and immaterial, like white-body Reason and Law, becomes operationalized according to the shifting needs of public normativity: order, accumulation, settler-colonialism, religious indoctrination, scape-goating, and so on. The abandoned body of the being without Reason is subject to the solicitation of rationalized subjection and metabolized into a vulnerability that is either too dispossessed to own political agency or overwhelmed by the necropolitical to exhibit life. Body outlines on asphalt tell the story of this abandonment. In the felt time of viral videos, its duration is 8'46". Autopsy reports are repurposed to further bury their abandoned voices in Reason.[3]

Poetry is capable of exorcising the ghosts from the process of exhuming the sensory, reanimating futures where the entire span of a person's life gets reduced and redacted down to a graphic form. Poetry infects the graphic form with fever. Poetry is what coughs from the dimensional limit of the graphic.

And it's in this reanimated *aesthesis* of graphia that I situate Douglas Kearney and Juno Morrow.

Poetics can unsettle the exceptionalism of language to represent itself purely or accurately as solely concerned with representing supremacist identity back onto the environment in a manner that substantiates supremacist liberalism. Rights. Or, as Christina Sharpe argues about "annotation in relation to the dysgraphia and the orthography of the wake," language between correct and incorrect expression exists in "relation to... photographs of Black people in distress that appear so regularly in our lives." The public "correctness" of rights against the unequal "incorrectness" in how rights are misapplied—reason and transgression rub people the wrong way. Poetic language of anger from this dysgraphia exists in relation to the ambient evidence, witnessed history, and felt experiences with rights. We exist in this moment in time in relation to the mediatization of this spectacle "whether the image of that suffering Black person comes from quotidian or extraordinary disasters, the photos of them often hit in the register of abandonment... even especially, when they purport to 'humanize'."[4]

In the neighborhood of thought, micha cárdenas, addressing trans necropolitics writes, "While visibility is managed by the algorithms of social media and communications networks, affect is the excess that seeps through these attempts at management. The affects of outrage and melancholy travel through social networks today in stories about the murder of [B]lack people and trans people of color."[5] Here cárdenas is referring specifically to affective contagion, which I underscored earlier as the manipulative and unethical experiment carried out by Facebook and Cornell University.[6] "Our necropolitical moment," writes cárdenas on the violence toward trans of color bodies, "is one in which horrific stories of the murders of people in our communities and families come to us daily through networked media.... If the primary tool of biopolitics was the census," she argues, invoking the work of the Achille Mbembe, "perhaps we can consider the paradigmatic tool of necropolitics to be the algorithm." The negativity cárdenas parses in this affective contagion is both description and agency in the algorithm, working through glimpses of pain exercised into the formula in our hands. This "time stamp" stands as a grotesque record of collective experience, and its unresponsive inhuman function teases at our wanting a less violent reality and our simultaneous ineffectiveness at convincing others not at risk that it should be so. When you work with archival history, as many poets today do, it's impossible to unsee how time-stamping algorithms date back to publics as a space of decision-making regarding Reason and Law in supremacist terms.

Sharpe is using the "wake" as a prolonged postapocalypse of bondage and operationalized governance in North America. There is a charge to things. Bodies carry a charge. Our bodies have been coded in that charge early on, far too early for any of us now to be guilty of the claims espoused by figures like Mather and others like him. There is still the matter of choice, however. And attention. I elicit a charge sometimes by just being in a room, a shared environment, a grocery store, my own back porch. When I'm around other bodies that produce kindred charges, I feel it. We nod. We speak. For some of us, our bodies are speech acts in and of themselves. This means there is a relationship to their being "public" that produces or defines this charge. But being public is also the charge to choose, which Mather underscores in his limited vocabulary for ethics. Sometimes being recognized for this charge by white-bodies occurs precisely in the complex arrangement of inclusion-by-abandonment. Abandonment is the decision to uphold an arcane public rationale. Abandonment is the weather, to use another of Sharpe's concepts, under which affective contagion spreads through the replication of violence and murder. What could poetry possibly offer, one might ask.

• • •

I have been focusing on affection and forms of touch that fall within the family of anger. I have been arguing that these demonstrations are demonstrations of knowing, which do not refer to a grasping, but open, instead, the possibility of postnational bonding. These demonstrations are also about knowing that does refer to living in a historical continuum and, if not grasping its logic, feeling its effects on how we conduct ourselves in that network of choices and reason dubbed "the public." In its coming to be, affective knowing travels through a vagal circuitry braiding bodies together through their injury into a collective assembly attentive to care, and that care is an old one through which anger works like butter-fuel to care about and care for abandoned persons. Sometimes that circuitry is a repetitive spitting out, a metabolic sweating. It's always a lot of fucking work.

Some need some Body
or more to ape sweat
on some site. Bloody

purl or dirty spit
hocked up for to show
who gets eaten. Rig

body up. Bough bow
to breeze a lazed jig
and sway to grig's good

fiddling. Pine-deep
dusk, a spot where stood
Body. Thus they clap

when I mount *banc'*, jig
up the lectern. Bow
to say, "it's all good,"

we, gathered, withstood
the bends of dives deep
er, darker. They clap

as I get down. Sweat
highlights my body,
how meats dyed bloody

look fresher for show
ing, I got deep, spit
out my mouth, a rig

id red rind. Bloody
melon. Ha! No sweat!
Joking! Nobody

knows the trouble. Rig
full o' Deus. "Sho
gwine fix dis mess." Spit

in tragedy's good
eye! "This one's called. . . ." Jig
ger gogglers then bow

housefully. They clap.[7]

Kearney walks the line of spectacularization, not to exploit its stage light, but as a ceremony tracing the boundaries of its gaze. He uncovers the boundary as a need for "some" to "need some Body / or more to ape Sweat," the stage of spectacularization being "some site. Blood," textured in a history of forced operationalization toward the laundering of liberalism through finance. Subjection laundered through the operationalization of Reason. Ceremony is sometimes an exorcism. Kearney is an exorcist. Kearney is also what I think of as a social geographer. His technique explores spatial relationships that include the obvious, the spectral, the lingering, and the charged. For those who've been to a Douglas Kearney reading, they would note the aural experience of voice as a demonstrative choreography of text design, and text design as a score with the scope and application of a map. Kearney's earlier books especially were graphically adventurous. Later books like *Sho*, I would argue, accomplish that experimentation in even more powerful ways of lyric demonstration. Audiences also get to experience the uncomfortable sense of humor Kearney volleys throughout the reading. A sense of humor that I often find to be explorative, seeking out the racism and skepticism, coaxing it out to expose it, tracing the boundaries of its hold on our attention.

I would argue there's something akin to patching at work. The patch in electronic music refers to a set of parameters through which an input sound is modulated toward an intentional effect. Originally, musicians had to physically "patch" synthesizers together using patch-cords, which routed signals through different hardware. Think of a telephone operator patching callers and receivers together. Now imagine that all the conversations taking place were in fact registers of one sonic body. Imagine that all the geography and distance and locations, all the stories and gossip and intimate whispers, all the news, all the fears and joys, were parameters a composer was not only aware of abstractly but was using in the precision of architecture or weaving toward the production of effects chained together in music. In contemporary music the patch is a function of coding and compressed hardware. The expansive network of patch-cords has been eliminated by the advent of digital memory.

Digital memory can store and disclose parameters at the will of the musician, at the push of a pad and slide of a knob.

A brief interlude through Herman Melville's "Donnelson" (1862).

> Of eager, anxious people met,
> And every wakeful heart was set
> On latest news from West or South.
> "No seeing here," cries one—"don't crowd—"
> "You tall man, pray you, read aloud."

The patch is a method of storing, briefly, memory for its disclosure in a social form. Music. The patch facilitates the speech act where spatiotemporally the control and efficacy of speech is least available, due either to distance or to pain, or to abstraction, memory loss, and so on. The crowd in one of my favorites of Melville's *Civil War Poems* comes together like starlings around the regular dispatches from the war. And the poem is rather experimental, kind of a proto-docupoetic work in how it incorporates news releases. It's the commentary from the crowd that is most fascinating to me because it holds together the event through acts of public contemplation regarding a shared site of collective experience. There are of course limitations, like the "tall man" exceptionalism. The patch exists as a solution to the colonial problem of access, and its technology ruptures borders in the space of the crowd, making available more information to more intellects, thereby expanding the physics of a public thinking around the speech act.

Speaking of crowds, "Thus they clap." "They need." I think of Baldwin: "I'm a man, but if you think I'm a ******, it means you need it."

I have been simultaneously processing the frustration that comes from being repeatedly told that one's perceptions of what is happening to one's own body are invalid. The poetic act is the demonstration of a critical environment for the body, wherein "Nobody / knows the trouble," and nobody knows the feeling, except those who do. Reaching out to this assembled community, the poetic utterance is also an uncovering of social banality that veils the condition, a critique of the state of exception scripted to privilege body-supremacy when it comes to the political valance of speech acts to call an assembly in the first place, persuade the assembly, move the assembly, guide the assembly. When we talk about the trouble, we aren't speaking for others, we're soothing the trouble that entire groups of us feel out, but which only some of us get a

FIGURE 13. Dancing, forever, forever dancing (Bo Jangles). Composition created from stills of Bill Robinson's "Stairs Dance," from "Harlem Is Heaven" (1932), directed by Irwin Franklin.

moment in history to articulate and point out. To be editorialized into silence is tantamount to being told truths are invalid or that the somatic reality of being bonded to others is not real. The political comes into view precisely at the bonding, a bonding complete with self-conscious observations, the chill of sweat and cold air, goosebumps and shivering, interlocked fingers.

Imagine this as a shared state of being in America—not intimated, but outright shared in the same networks through which we share reels of funny panda antics, or photos of our children, other peoples' children, bichons in funny clothes. This frustration is a particularly volatile frustration when it is white bodies, as authorities of the perceptible, that refuse to acknowledge the truth of perceptible events their neuroses create in and *as* the shared atmosphere we call "publics," even while white choices, white selections, white *purchases* help shape the very same algorithms through which decolonial acts are communicated following violence. Kearney's work takes this one step farther and into the shared somatic space of pilomotor reflexes and stimuli. The speaker in "Sho" is the agent marking the space of the "show," cognizant of the "body," cognizant of the performative gestures of "getting down" off the stage and how "they clap / as I get down." "I get down," as in lay it out, but it's also the moment immediately after. Kearney's is a fleshy poetics of expenditure in our precise historical moment of contagion. This is the risk and the weight of reward. Fleshiness is how some of us interact with the world: our flesh, the flesh like ours. We cry into our phone screens. We look for comfort in the very information that validates our injury. The best we can do is mark our arms with the bruises of kin.

Sara Ahmed's realization that "when we give problems their names, we can become a problem for those who do not want to talk about a problem" describes how this frustration is partly felt for those of us who both embody positional subjectivity and operate inside institutions of critique, like academe.[8] This is especially so because academe preserves rules and dispositional expectations when it comes to critique, namely that there should be disciplinary boundaries between somatic writing and citational networking. Poetry, as I am contextualizing its vatic act, invites listening, patching, and re-remembering as a necessarily somatic-cognitive attention.

"Sho" is written in a form one of his students invented and dubbed, torchon, which incorporates aspects of sestina but with adaptations to woven patterns using words not lines. When one sees/hears Kearney read this woven pattern the experience can be an informational cascade. The repetition of words like "Sho/Show," "bloody," "body" exist in a landscape of sensory knowledge that operates somewhere between closure, stress, strain, and abolition. The text itself exists somewhere between dysgraphia and orthographic representation, to use Christina Sharpe's analysis of image "in the wake." By dysgraphia I don't mean an incorrectness under a universal correction of expression, but rather an unsettled source of information from an event traveling back and forth between emergence and acknowledgement. Dysgraphia is what we experience when we read Cotton Mather's sermons in the twenty-first century. It's the purposeful difference-virological susceptibility between "get down" and "get down," a "show" and "to show," "bloody" and "body," the grammar in lyric like "fiddling," "Pine-deep / dusk, a spot where stood / Body. Thus they clap." You can't read "Pine-deep" without being transported to a nineteenth-century scene of subjection, fugitivity, or murder, not if you've read anything from the nineteenth century, or the early twentieth. Not if you've read Toomer's *Cane*. Not if you have ever heard of Versie Johnson or the Piney Woods of Mississippi. Not if you live in the world.

Dysgraphia is about ghosts as much as it is about literacy or fluency. And living with those ghosts is a different experience for different folks existing in different generational timelines. But this is the turn I'm hoping to get to by the time we attend to Divya Victor and Claudia Rankine's somatic, gestational poetics in *Curb* and *Plot,* respectively. Intergenerational, transgenerational, or inherited trauma, as national dysgraphia, is not the demonstration of a dysfunction or deficit in the soma, but shared responses to systemic white-body supremacy in America as a nation of publics woven together by exceptionalism, and the heritage of American togetherness as a practice of supremacy in the face of changes to voice, property, citizenship, and freedom. America's unwavering politics and cultural fragility exhibits a consciousness that depends on exceptionalism, bodies that depend on this belief as if it were life itself.

• • •

The relationship I am drawing here with Kearney's work and the work of Juno Morrow is with visibility, publics, and fleshiness. A demonstration of embodiment in the face of exceptionalist consciousness that must find its place on the page, given the limitations and potentiation the page offers, that is, composition. Both writers produce highly designed texts that are clearly circuited into the mediatized environment where culture informs itself. My interest is in that place where public and lyric confront one another as modes of existing textually or algorithmically (in that the algorithm potentially replaces active reading under certain conditions of attention/lessness). Existing archivally, being documented, the design of thought unfolds plastically in a medium that also represents the potential of politics as a promise that the public brings into being. A poetry doesn't editorialize affect but heightens its existence in the historical context, and this includes, maybe particularly, textually innovative poetics.

Anger, like meteors, is also marvelous. It evidences our existence in time. It's not the only attribute—being affective and sentient creatures—that does this. Anger implies a great deal of thoughtfulness toward understanding how relationality, itself, functions. This curiosity, or what we call attention, is also wonderful. In recent years, attention has been targeted as a demonstration of the reductive "wokeness" that marks bodies exhibiting anger as illegitimately social. Not their exclusion, to be clear. But the inclusion of consciousness toward the disqualification of a historically conscious state. And yet, we continue paying attention to history.

Holler at us, vecinos. Who "move along"? When there
is nothing to see here, we're there.[9]

Here is a speculative methodology: many readers will instantly connect Kearney's poetics to an event, possibly multiple events, from their own experience. I like to think of this connection as a poetics, a ¡vecino! poetics. I remember once as a child walking through our neighborhood after dinner and coming upon an intersection in front of a popular liquor store called Purple Cow, which had a larger-than-life-sized cartoonish purple cow in front that would get stolen and returned every so often. A child on a skateboard had just been struck by a car running a stop sign. The skateboard had rolled to a stop against the curb where my family stood next to other vecinos, and the sunset washed over us, and the scene gradually exposed more and more glass and detailed fragments on the asphalt that began to shimmer as night settled. We saw more the less sunlight we could rely on. The flashing cadence of the ambulance spoke of urgency, a vast and widening strobe with each blink, though it felt overall ubiquitous. I remember my pilomotor reflex syncing to the crowd in an indescribable way, as if we were flowers talking to each other pheromonally, seemingly silently, passing along information from petal to petal, using the breeze to feel connected. We had gathered there, all of us who were there, and made a "here" out of it. Belonging to a moment, a negative moment that escapes any sort of narrative or framework for making sense of it, lives in the skin and observation. Paying attention ignites a charge, a reflex and disorientation. Attention improvises orientation and grounding through the patchwork of sensations and self-defense hormones that ready one's body to survive. Moments like these, which are jarring, are also moments that need a forensic attention, and forensic information must find its way into the public again lest it be lost to the dust of archives. Text is part of this process.

Posdnous does not mean to spectacularize human trafficking, chattel genocide, or racialized violence with the meteor as metaphor, with his invocation of rights and the meteor's implicit sovereignty where Black bodies have not had this privilege. But he brings us to these scenes by invoking the forensics; as a metaphor this matrix of meanings and demonstration, touching, implication, and sovereignty carries the weight of anger over into the knowledge of public sense. So too does Kearney's lyric speaker and their sensing the stage. So too does Morrow and her sensing the boundary of her body and its social environment. How could it not?

Someone might object to or refuse the resemblance Posdnous draws, and maybe even be angered by the imposition of witnessing the ethical dilemma implied by the scene, triggered by listening. But incarnating the dilemma is not the same thing as draping the spectacle of dissent over voice toward accomplishing visibility.[10] Incarnating the dilemma in a ceremony with ¡vecinos! is maybe closer to a ritual of sensible exhumation. Metafora, Cecilia Vicuña wrote decades ago, from *metapherin*, is "to bear across... to carry over into."[11] This will resonate. Suffice it to say from the outset and in the hemispheric context, which is our North American context, to "bear across" emerged at one point centuries ago as an existential worldmaking necessitating the actual building of a material territory. Our modernity was both extraterrestrial—unfathomable in the technological disequilibrium of force and violent consequence—and erected on terrestrial, very corporeal genocide.[12] I am not talking about a generalized or phenomenological anger, or simply referring to a capacity for anger. A poetics of anger delves into an affective worldmaking the way love is important. And what I want to stress is that this anger belongs to all of us in the way our shared situation imbeds cultural lessons along hormonal pathways, coding behaviors according to a vast but focused system. ¡Vecino! is code for assembly. We aren't born with beliefs. We share them with our neighbors, especially when confronted with apocalyptic discomfort. ¡Vecino! is a way of existing in an attention to assembly.

> We are expected to encapsulate so much of our identities and experiences in what we call ourselves. Claiming an identity feels impossible when no one sees you as you are. Those that slice their experiences thin are often dismissed as dismissive or self-involved. Labels create boundaries as much as they create community. Still, we strive to find our place in a world of borders.[13]

A poetics of anger does more than impart anger instructionally, which is perhaps more akin to a poetry of protest. I'm underscoring a different speech act. One that introduces a kind of thinking that happens through the disclosure of emotional content in a publicly available form, which within its own parameters also improvises its relationship to audience—reconstituting that which makes a coincidental geographic assembly into a public, as it's been promised to us. Anger is a residue feeling. In Juno Morrow's lyric memoir, the frustrated tension in identity as a simultaneously liberatory promise and a threatening social contract discloses this kind of anger. It is in the grammar, the violence of an archival identity of "experiences" sliced "thin," down to irrefutable facts that nevertheless are disqualified as "divisive or self-involved," anyway. Morrow's is a lyric body pressed against a thinking-reflecting collective cortex.

Vatic anger that cites a historical scene in the present tense of lyric address is complex because the speaker assumes a collective recipient while anticipating as well as disavowing reception to the speech act. For ¡vecinos! in the crowd there is a resemblance of both what is witnessed as well as the anticipated response from those who refuse to witness. This is what makes poetry of anger so intricately fascinating. It remains forward calling, anticipatory, informed, and often even cites evidence. Yet even where some in the audience recognize the credibility of sourcing, poetry of anger does not prescriptively disavow spaces for the white-body exceptionalism that will inevitably show itself. It doesn't exclude exceptionalism. It welcomes it into the competing logic of consciousness and empathy, of ethics and civility toward presenting to audience the work of civic discernment. There, exposed, exceptionalism runs of out of the calories it must feed on. We all find ourselves in poetry, in a microcosm of historical dilation, and the work there is to examine the corpse of exceptionalism.

At the center of these assertions is how I am framing "publics." Is it a description of kinds of relationships and the matrices through which relationships fan out across materialities, affinities, and human affect? Or is the term "public" a set definition to which the latter elements must adhere? Morrow introduces another option as a negotiation of sorts on the verso page. The recto is a full-sized magenta-tinted portrait of the author, head cocked sideways, a left hand hanging above the ear as if about to press gently through the membrane of the page. Her hair brings a border of black to the portrait. And just where it ends in the bottom left corner in soft curls, a blue background is exposed in the slightest of fractal geometry. Morrow is a self-declared hybrid. Hybrid is a word we use, a label. It offers possibility. It creates boundaries. Hybrid is a negotiation, and negotiations are limited speech acts that reveal where we are and are yet unwilling to go. As far as consensus, it performs a spectacularized ethics of relation. The arcane territories of Reason and Law built on fear, uncertainty, difference, and the comforting allure of likeness. As someone whose work is sometimes called hybrid, I understand the reliance on the ability of a metaphor to carry us beyond the boundary of uncertain outcome. For me hybridity is a result of impulse control issues. But the tricky reality that we carry in our national, public weight keeps this an interesting visual, like Lite Brite, a toy from the '80s, but seen not how they looked in ads, but how they lived in peoples' homes, with missing lights and as if they were themselves self-animated, falling or moving across the black board in patterns clearly missing pieces but generally with a shared direction.

Metaphor serves an imaginative, creative purpose. If creative refers to the space of illumination as the silent stillness from which noise emerges, what has been lost of late is the role imaginative labor plays in sustaining the human world as a creative experience, particularly where the imaginative ethics of care or public love builds a purposeful human world. Why is a reticence to the ways a certain kind of poetry demonstrates anger received as an affront to Reason as the sole Law of aesthetic beauty? Metaphorical thinking helps us understand the difference between beneficence and nonmaleficence as a basic starting point toward communal health work. The difference is between an exceptionalist belief in a fictional, complete individual bestowed with a social stewardship versus the understanding that we, all of us, have work to do toward a constituted environment. An attention to our incompleteness, to the ingredients that are before us, but the outcome is an idea only. The metaphor is a carrying over. Living with this poetry teaches us how this work binds us generationally to public historical realities. We meet in those historical moments through direct witness or familial stories. We are bound to each other, for better or worse, and it takes a great deal of work to understand exactly how. The payoff is shared. Collective. The health is communal, even if painful to relive. Even when it's "over," what holds us requires care and attention.

> My face takes on inclines and angles as I look back, recognizing how much I've lost. Once again, I order shady pills from the internet, this time from India. I hope to walk back the dysphoria, slowing my descent into an ever more masculine form. I think to myself that maybe if I can treat the symptoms to control my dysphoria, I can go forever without really having to address who I am.[14]

The demos in the North American imaginary seeks to exist freely, but the demos must also rely on the nonmaleficence of the human world for not being subsumed but granted a sensible sovereignty to continue being not a showpiece. What this means and why I stress nonmaleficence instead of beneficence is that the steep and exponential "descent" Morrow feels her way through is influenced by the external Reason and Law through which relationality garners consequence by attaching itself to dominant forms of embodied being that resonate most strongly with a masculinity that is also the least self-assuredly somatic, and therefore the most likely to attack any variation that threatens the androcentric cultural fiction it adheres to. There is a much graver consequence than mere survival for one body, in that utterance unravels the whole structure. In this exponent overwhelm it's not so much about survival in the evolutionary sense, but survival in the survivalist sense of surviving socially permissible and moralistically operationalized predation.

While the demos functions through principles as well as practices, there must be a constant reflection on how principles induce dysphoria, and how practices operationalize the human response to dysphoria as a somatic strain to literally see oneself as one is through the social veil of how the features one owns are prescribed cultural and social value. Value, in a neoliberal and capitalist sense is necropolitical enough. When we factor in the racialized necropolitics of America, or how transphobia expresses implicit fears of sexual uncertainty for cismasculine white bodies as chosen "settlers" of American terrain and people, both sexually speaking and patriarchically speaking (and the specific transphobia directed at children), we arrive at the consideration of factors that open pathways toward empathy at the embodied level of feeling Morrow's "hope," Morrow's "looking back," her loss, her "forever." I'm not saying *we know* this. I'm saying I feel this through the layer of affect Morrow textures into that which I recognize as poetics. We think through our bodies. Our bodies are built to understand poetry. A poetry of negativity reminds us why this is so, in responding to the whole of what our bodies are apt to make public in their design to relate. Because we also care through our bodies about something rather primitive and essential: survival. It's important to build our democratic publics. It's more important that we survive our democratic publics.

• • •

As neighbors in these publics, it's important that we understand the communicability of pain as potential for affective contagion and that we therefore understand the difference between clean pain and dirty pain. Both Morrow's and Kearney's are clean pain, an intelligent pain, which I mean to describe as a thoughtful, thinking pain. It is informed by history and aware that actions script history.

That my sweat, alchemical—
of shit, makes gold? Factual.

Consider spent plantation dirt,
arena turf, recording booth—
what transmogrifies these
sans my properties?

If it could it should it's been bottled?[15]

A poetry of anger is poetry of the event, not the spectacularization of what eventing brings forth into the spotlight. A ¡vecino! poetics is a careful poetics that demonstrates attention through structuring attention aesthetically, formalistically. That the lyric speaker here is both in the spotlight and aware of the alchemy, "my sweat" reorients the nexus of body, expenditure, and light. Kearney highlights the "factual," the historical, as the public history under scrutiny. This reorientation disassembles the focal systems that frame individual experience and expression as subjective interpretations, leaving bare the dominant expectation for listening to non-Reasonable bodies. This expectation erects two impasses: the progressive/academic diminishment of pain into a fungible, less somatically dimensional display (of intellectualized pain for a Reason-informed, Law-abiding audience audience), and/or the anti-Black refusal to acknowledge virtuosity, speech, or sentience (the disavowal of Black intelligence at the site of Black feeling).

The embodiment of anger in Kearney's lyric anticipates both forms of indignity, which are, in their extension toward a shared space of experience, performances of safety in the face of Black citizenship, if what we consider citizenship to be is having access to shape a collective consciousness built from language that exhibits negativity and discomfort of attending to clean pain. Menakem makes the distinction between "clean" and "dirty" pain as pain that is identified and dealt with and pain that is "blown through" other bodies.[16] The YouTube commenter @KevinoftheCosmos, for instance, exhibits dirty pain when they blow through Kearney with their individual, unprocessed anger, stating "I imagine a bunch of rich white people gathered to listen to this saying 'Oh my god, exceptional.' and 'So visceral, so cathartic!' But not a single one saying 'What absolute idiocy.'" When they wonder "out loud" why no good ole' American present had the bravery to put Kearney in his place.

Kearney's pain utilizes this expectation of fragility-turned-hate, and the collective experiences of Black America to propose a trauma that needs collective attention. He premeditates it as much as a poet is capable of premeditating the reading of love or joy. Imagine the two radically different publics in each circuit of pain.

Imagine which is better suited for us to connect the dots and disentangle the communicability of exploitation hoisted onto Black performance and expenditure through—which is more suited to white-body supremacy? It is individual in the sense of Kearney being a Black man in America, a partner, a father, a son, a teacher, and an archivist of experiences, yet also vatic in the ways the individual pain is shared with others toward verifying its existence, first and foremost. The demonstration of this sovereignty starts with a sovereignty from one's own pain, from one's own ghosts, redefines the public through a re-examination of definition or fatalism, and the aesthetic reorientation of descriptions of public existence toward validating a public somatically. Doing so refuses the spectacularization of the body in its vulnerable state of being exposed in its feeling within colonial parameters. It's the self-awareness of one's "properties," as well as the historical context within which those properties have been determined according to colonial logic. I want to stress that this includes white bodies in a vulnerable state, like commentor @KevinoftheCosmos.[17] There is, however, some truth to this observation, that the "rich white people," which I gather refers to those privileged by class and education, would quickly praise Kearney's work but not engage with its sentience. It's almost a challenge between white-body neuroses to not permit Black experience or Black reflection to enter the commons. In the former there is hatred and an unwillingness to share the demos; in the latter there is guilt and an unwillingness to share the in-process work of exorcising America's past.[18]

> We need our stories to humanize difference in both others and ourselves. Complexly realized identities are difficult to abbreviate, often assumed to be the worst by those unwilling to listen. They say the safest way to navigate a dangerous place is to look like you know where you're going, stuttering is seen as weakness, making us vulnerable to the desires and ideas of others.[19]

Morrow touches on safety with care of a body made unsafe in America. Remembering that you can also be unsafe in spontaneous ways, like the child we, as vecinos, hoped for yet gazed through in front of Purple Cow years ago, safety as a logistic, or planning for the Lawfulness of a public needs to be unpacked for the ways it governs relationality through learning values as the operational benefit of ideas. A poetry of anger is about relation as a site of public knowledge through shared process, not the spectacularization of historical lessons about the "safest" way of being in the presence of others. Morrow's lyric speaker underscores something about "safety" I haven't unpacked yet, which is how it is both a social concept referring to a signifier-stability and a somatic necessity. As such, "difference" as reverberating experiences between safety and something "other," not as threat but other enough to be perceived as such, "isn't dishonesty, but a representation of the relationality of identity."[20]

Trauma needs to be understood in relation to "safety," and both in the context of American relationality. While we may dress them in narrative, something our brains do over time, especially with the assistance of external reinforcement and learning, trauma is in fact bodily. It is somatic, as I have been arguing. Living in the body, trauma finds expression through reactions to perceptions of threat. In the Americas threat has been inculcated into our judicial, carceral, educational, medical, legislative, and sexual institutions, to name some of the most prominent systems instituted in colonial settlement. When the body is permitted, and encouraged, in fact, to respond to fears in a manner that benefits social order as well, the somatic network in our bodies and the primitive bean called the lizard brain are allowed to sit behind the wheel, so to speak. The amygdala is the processing center of our limbic system, through which we process emotions. But this processing is not intellectual. Trauma, reminds Menakem, "is all about speed and reflexivity." Trauma is a way of understanding survival, but "traumatic retention," how trauma has been stored in our bodies in unaddressed ways, manifests as very specific kinds of dysfunction that blur the lines where our bodies and our identities approach one another.

We can give these dysfunctional and maladaptive convergences of learning and reflex names: white supremacy, racism, transphobia and homophobia, misogyny, xenophobia, ableism, and more broadly speaking demonstrations against expansive definitions of life that refuse to corroborate with white-body exceptionalism. Our bodies "act as if the danger is real" no matter what, while our lizard brains have been educated about the danger from the dominant narratives authored by supremacist ideology under the disguise of exceptionalism. Why? Because supremacist ideology in the Americas has historically used safety and security as their primary poetics.

In "Do the Backseat Jam!" Kearney braids the pacification of Black performance in Mather's conversion supremacy to the overwhelming permissibility of fear-governed force—on Black bodies, for example.

> Stop there fam and jump to the brand spanking
> back again you how it go throw your hands
> in the air when the lights on maestro raise the baton
> and swing till you feel it the beat what's taking over
> the street to the club when I say you say *ow*[21]

In Kearney's performance, voice, register, and address intersect around the back and forth of embodiment as a public text of national sense. Annotation, dysgraphia, and somehow the implicit necessity remains that a body survive, that a public be in its innate existence somehow purposeful in a manner that aligns practice and belief and that we are somehow supposed to not know about history. Or under the assumption that maybe we don't have phones in our hands capable of bringing noise to our ears that makes us want to dance as well as images of kin on the floor. Kearney's and Morrow's poetics openly reflect on what lives in the body. Their work underscores the body as an archive of transgenerational memory, thought, and expression—literally the processes of language born out of permissible, commodified, denied, or mal/adaptive demonstrations of expressed need. The connection I am making in poetry is one that bridges somatic health as tended to by therapists like Menakem and speech acts as demonstrations of affective and limbic needs that exceed individual process because the origin of their systemic disruption lies in a historical event that only part of the living community acknowledges. Thus, I am not just talking about Black bodies in Kearney's work, or trans bodies in Morrow's, but also about the other bodies reinforcing, confronting, or internalizing white-body supremacy through their participation in linguistic and demonstrative publics.

If I return to the question of what is a public, maybe it's the duration of attention. Consider, from *con-sidereal*, together with the stars, a temporalization of an imaginary exertion that describes the phenomenal experience of looking up into the stretch of universe above, as what also defines the human condition of *looking up, together.*

• • •

In the summer of 1991, a nine-year old child named L—— A—— was abducted from her family's apartment and brutally killed. Near where her body was found, the community began reporting the image of a woman's visage on an empty billboard situated just south of a dirt parking lot and a fruit stand where my mom often stopped. I loved the way this fruit stand smelled. The fruit stand was in a sort of residential-commercial sluice made of silty contaminated runoff, reeds, and goat head thorn bushes. All along the coastal acres of San Diego one finds estuaries that melt into a similar sandy turbulence. In some parts of the city these are revered spaces, often photographed and cared for. The farther south one goes, the less attention these estuaries receive, at least a kind of considerate attention. I find this odd because there's something more impossibly aesthetic about an egret posing in its hunt for fast-moving calories amidst the wreckage of neglect than peacefully fishing in the "beauty" of environmental exception.

These estuaries cut deep into the landscape along escarpments. They are ancient.

The fruit stand was at the base of such an escarpment where South-South San Diego, where I lived, became Chula Vista, a larger, more commercially and residentially robust town often associated with what is called the South Bay. L's body was found in the brambly wet landscape between the escarpment and the fruit stand. And so Our Lady of Chula Vista, as the apparition came to be called, chose the billboard beside the dirt lot, beside a small fruit stand, near smelly trash-littered marsh oozing under an overpass. It all made reasonable sense. It became impossible to get fruit. They started charging for the parking lot as more and more believers flocked to see the image of a woman's face. Some saw three faces. Some saw two faces. Some say it was L. Some just saw La Virgen. We went once early in the phenomenon. It was nighttime and people were handing out little white candles with paper bases, like the kind one gets during processions of La Virgen de Guadalupe. I remember standing with other people holding a little candle. I think I was wearing a karate gi, because maybe we had stopped by after practice. (My brother had been obsessed with joining karate, and being fifteen months apart, I got roped into it also.) The sweat on my face and across my back felt refreshing yet dry also. The dust from the fields around us swirled from the traffic of cars. Their warm motors radiated into our circles and crowded assemblies as they slowed and veered over to the side of the road, gazed, and sped away up the escarpment. Nights like this one and the night at Purple Cow are memorable to me. They trigger something familiar. People standing close to each other, maybe in silence, maybe conferring with what they've just witnessed. People standing, trying to make sense of something that, given the incomprehensibility of history in North America, because of its violent origins, they have been trained to do. These assemblies are spontaneous, but they seem as unavailable as any other assembly, given how they converge.

If anything, one might glean from experiences like this that there is no way to stay safe. But that's not what I remember. Or at least, that's not how I remember being around others at night when goosebumps and softness speak, when resilience is the insistence of little candles and billboard lights against darkness. There's an important way to pay attention together when safety is made vulnerable. Experimental poetics attempts to recreate this same kind of temporary attention by leaving the shore of certainty and canon.

I'm walking a fine line between spectacularization and epistemology, perhaps merely performing without insight into the choreography, without knowing the movements. I am between being mesmerized and without footing, allowing the sublime to sour into resentment, shame, or jealousy, and appreciating deeply where movements come from and what orbits they illustrate in digestible, recognizable forms and sensation. Key here, if I patch in De La Soul, is the meteor. Lonely and extraterrestrial, yet more terrestrial perhaps than, say, a Pez dispenser, or a Super PAC, the meteor asks a question of its environment about how it will be incorporated into its memory. Let me change the signal in the patch for a beat.

> no debemos olvidar que la modernidad, desde sus inicios hasta hoy, ha estado constituida por una matriz estructural que, en su despliegue, genera diferentes formas de colonialidad, subordinación y exclusión, entre ellas la colonialidad del poder, la colonialidad del ser, la colonialidad de la naturaleza y la colonialidad de la sensibilidad. Esta última, como colonialidad de lo sensible, se despliega en especial a través de los regímenes del arte y la estética que hacen parte de la expansión de la matriz colonial de la modernidad, en un abanico de formas mediante las cuales se pretende, más allá del exclusivo espacio del arte, abarcar la totalidad de los ámbitos de la vida.[22]

[let's not forget that modernity, since its inception to today, has been constituted by a structural matrix, which in its disposition generates different forms of colonialism, subordination and exclusion, within them the colonialization of power, of being, the colonialization of nature and the senses. This last example, the colonialization of the sensible, is carried out in particular through art and aesthetic regimes that form part of the outgrowth of those modernist matrices, fanning out in substructures that, more than simply providing the spaces of art, encompass the totality of scopes of life. (*Translation mine.*)]

While entertaining, patching is a function of memory is a function of decolonializing spaces is a function of assembling the affective excess that emanates from "the totality of scopes of life." Sensible experiences are made truly possible through being enhanced as elements of storytelling that can potentially decolonize these "scopes of life" in that they live in us as memories, as well as through the learned repertoires through which we are made public. I am talking about simple and radical border crossing: spontaneous, impromptu, as demonstrative of a relationship to audience. Acts come from a world wherein the actors are aware of historical valance.

To experience storytelling in Mignolo's critique is to reenact the communal experience of human connection that comes from listening to place ourselves in a space of spontaneity where safety and unforeseen change coexist, maybe too close for Reason to keep track of. Then the body simply takes over, and maybe this is ok. To know we must sense in a way, and be sensed, knowledge has to demonstrate itself, openly. It's a tricky alchemy that poetry frames in its technique, because we are surrounded by information daily and occupy mediated environments through which we experience our "scopes of life." Especially in feeling in control of choosing those environments, we unknowingly fan the affective contagion of a futureless future.

In the Midwest, the murder of George Floyd brought neighborhoods together across farmlands, prairie, and marshlands. Soundwaves and social media posts floated over the ghostly footprints of migration and sandhill crane families, rippled over ancient lakes, and rattled the spring chunks of wet asphalt still coated in crystalline ice in "small town" intersections like the ones just a few miles south from where I sit thinking about the importance of poetry in processing an anger that might produce a more genuine democracy. I'm a vecino. I have vecinos an hour and a half away across the St. Croix in Minnesota, where there is an entire city block dedicated to preserving the anger and sadness of losing a family member. Throughout the Midwest and beyond people put their bodies on the ground where they stood and performed an act called lie-ins. Students at my university did this also along our modest quad. We are meant to reply to precarity with the display of vulnerability as an act of solidarity, which is also a decision to understand. It's exactly when there's "nothing to see here" that there is reason to see, to truly see. Not spectate but witness. This is a key distinction in avoiding spectacularization. It is a cognitive awareness of one's "properties" and the history and logistics of how they are displayed for sale. We can intervene in those logistics but that requires studying them and working through the mess that builds from abuse and exploitation. The mess that accumulates into an impossible future sabotages one's ability to move, and see, and breathe, and otherwise makes it just easier to surrender.

I want to underscore that to surrender is not the exhibition of pathology, but the outcome of design. How many times can we toss these hot-potato terms back and forth before someone finally gives up and utters chicharros?

dreams

I dream about spiders. They are large, beautiful, deeply black spiders. On their abdomens there is a bright red symbol. My dream-brain calls them black widows, but the symbol is not an hourglass. These spiders don't overwhelm. They don't crowd my body or crawl on my skin. I don't have to shake them off. They don't suffocate. They don't dampen the oxygen around my mouth or nose like fire. They are serene. They are still. I am the one who approaches them. I feel a flush of adrenaline when I do. This adrenaline is not fear, but an arousal. A sensory inflammation throughout my dream-body preparing to move. Anticipating movement even. It is the coming alive of the parts of my dream-skin feeling out new atmosphere, like a lightly wet sponge being breathed on by hundreds of little fluttering seeds. My nerves settle into the reassurance that I am spatial, my tissue into a welcoming cushion of the impulsive "not yetness" that awaits at the culmination of a process.

Body and mind relate through sensation and predictive worldmaking. My body and mind extend from the nurturing web of dreams. Language plays a role in the dilation of my awareness in the haptic directions of what I perceive. I am talking about a kind of language the purpose of which is to uncover. A kind of language that exists prior to operation, prior to capital, prior to exploitation, or relation-as-power. Language massages arousal as an inflammation back into the tissue. Anger, being expressive, and expression a swelling of signals in the immediate space between, anger is also clarity. As emotions are. But though they clarify, it is also unclear what they are. Anger is an excess of sensation produced as a byproduct to speech where it blooms only to be mitigated by the logic of the social in our postapocalyptic expectation that bodies must suffer through the historical. The thwarting of creative action in the face of resolving historical problems hurts. It becomes anger when the sensations from preparing to face reenactments returns to a somatic core only to realize how the origins of this mitigating, operational logic are a construct oriented by and masked as exceptionalisms. This individual experience can be mapped and corroborated.

I have been arguing that we can feel through others. I've been feeling through the others that are here as poetic voice, lyric utterance, vatic address. We can know what others feel by feeling, ourselves. That is only part of cultural adaptation. Language can be used "to inquire into our tendency to place language as the determinant of experience," as Erin Manning puts it.[1] We are brought into personhood as a container of complex processes we can, if pressed or if we exhaust metaphor, whittle down to nervous activity, racing thoughts, flashing sensations. As the poets I read throughout this book acknowledge in their futurist calls, however, the architecture undergirding the shared spaces and meaningful publics where process builds and dilutes the person are colonial in origin. Supremacist in intent, even. If emotions clarify, but we are unclear as to their authority in publics, what governs the economy of our attention to them? What hierarchy of care do we consent to and how was it derived? Whatever nihilation is possible becomes operationalized by the dehumanizing "determinant" of exploitation as the "experience" of reality. And yet there is poetry from this stressful state of arousal and swollen signals, emotions, and hapticity.

Dreams and memories, as shimmers of what is left over and unresolved, offer a pause on sensation by heightening the dilation between the felt, the anticipated, and the ideated. Poetry can exploit this loophole in us, and often poets can intentionally enter dilation through performing their practice. I'm talking about poets who integrate performance into their compositional practice like Divya Victor and micha cárdenas. Their performatic ethos appears to be a direct engagement with the nightmare often called the American dream, and these poets feel their way through its haunting parallax via their bodies. When I say performance I am referring to "disclosure" in the original term. The act of "carrying out" or the "coming true" of the act or event is rather closely aligned with Cecilia Vicuña's framing of metaphor as a "carrying over." I'm not talking about entertainment, which would become the prominent use of the word in the eighteenth century. I am talking about the performance of creating a "body one can live with" as cárdenas writes in the media-lyric work "Pregnancy," which interrogates the promise of translatina gestation and the "performance" of gender-futurity via the necessity of hormone therapy.

Settling the arousal of dysphoria, hormonal utterance shapes the sensations coming true of a body in an anti-genocidal futurity against the mitigating social influences of necropolitical transphobic and racialized violence.

In "Pregnancy," cárdenas gives lyric voice to the diurnal transformations of hormone replacement therapy juxtaposed to a microscopic focus on the motility and health of her sperm cells. In fact, the poems were written during a period wherein the artist went off hormones to bring her body's sperm count into "normal" range. This physiological re/orientation cárdenas calls "shifting." "By shifting my body's state," writes cárdenas in a postscript, "I was able to produce new knowledges, and new material output."[2] In producing new knowledge at the site of the body, literally the cellular site of her gametes, the poem's complicated relationship to contentment and "mattering" discloses unique knowledge for the reader as well. Not a spectacularization of "transition," shifting underscores the materially cultural significance of sensations between somatic adaptations, social critique of transphobia, and the cultural potential of linear futurity as spiracle, more haptically linear than linear in the binary sense of start-to-finish. The diaryesque, linear lyric is given over to ongoing refraction, an *aesthesis* from the cellular outward, into the sociocultural dimension. Gender-as-construct and gender-as-survival draw an equally microscopic focus on the health of the body within which the disclosed sperm cells must also survive. Where they must thrive marks the kairotic imperative that culture thrive as well as the futurial holding environment where the lives, "multitudes," in her cells will live.

"[H]ow many people are inside me?" she ponders in the video installation version of "Pregnancy," between zoomed in and slowed down images of her microscope view into slides containing a growing and motile density of gametes.[3]

I hate testosterone,

> there are many reasons why I take estrogen
> and spironolactone to block my testosterone.
> I feel the edge back in my mind,
> the edge of impatience, of being quick to anger,
> the old version of myself seeps in,
> in my voice, which sounds so deep and strange to me.[4]

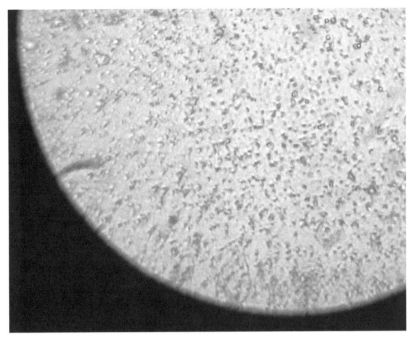

FIGURE 14. "Pregnancy," video by micha cárdenas, 2017.

Noting "anger" in relation to a "quickness," cárdenas maps the sensory and perceiving state of masculinist social liberty and socialized disposition. Her disposition toward "liberty" as the liberty to one's own cellular life implicates in its very emotionality the public transphobic social desire to erase bodies that do not align with the white Christian national model of person. Some might note in the faces on social media or news feeds that scowling white cis-gendered protesters perform a similar shape to "anger." But these faces operate in the dysregulated freedom to take up space. Theirs is a hatred. Hate isn't about liberty as much as it is an obsession with a nonexistent eugenic principle undergirding the cultural exceptionalism of "national" space. Hate rides the wave of dissatisfaction that comes from the disclosing of delusion.

Supremacy, via exceptionalism as a socialized belief system that organizes bodies, has exploited the aspect of language that bids us to listen, to address, in order to supplant collectivity with the contagion of "influence." So they end up looking similar, but are not. "Culture is stored in populations," write Boyd and Richerson, "understanding human brains and how populations change requires a population thinking."[5] But population thinking is not the same as eugenic assumption-making when it comes to positioning non-white and "non-normative" bodies in relation to a fantasized supremacy that is designed to maintain a monopoly on the observable universe and the locative desire to center human experience in that universe. Working backward from assemblies, like population, like culture, we are reintroduced to fundamental ways our bodies exist in time, as well as the ways we come to assemble and come to believe in culture in an almost evolutionary desire to be safe, to control for threat, or to accumulate resource. Culture is a repository of creative acts and creative potential. Social influences outline imitative behaviors.

Despite this difference we are constantly being challenged to believe in culture as an accumulated archive of supremacist facticity. This is called a culture war. It describes attempts to burn or ban books, revise history, use model minorities to underwrite supremacist ideas. We are taught to believe in the evolutionary truth of white-body supremacy through axioms that align, in their fantastical logic, bodily exceptionalism and democratic culture. I was taught this throughout public school, and it made us hate ourselves for not being implicitly represented in the world, which we understood to be a public demonstration of acceptance. Bodily exceptionalism relies on the sort of patterning that has less to do with adaptive influences learned through confrontation than it is an operationalization of relationality toward the imitation and reenactment of ideology. The social influence of bodily exceptionalism is replication, which has less to do with care, or intimacy, than it does with atomization, and positional predation. Care is a fundamental adaptive event, a cultural resource. Care is not always far from forms of lyricizing anger. Care is a form of attention that makes the temporality of lyric "valuable." Care is a fundamental safety response. Poetry is care in the shape and tenor of address.

These spiders though.

I find these dream-spiders outside whatever dream-house my dream-self is occupying. Usually by doors: front door, back door. Sometimes they are near windows. They are, to be fair to them, always outside the house. They are very prominently built, these spiders. Robust bodies, an extraterrestrial magnitude of color that seems impossible in our spectrum. Mystic, bear-pelt-like. A matte surface impossible of reflection. Without reflection, a surface capable of

FIGURE 15. Abuelos con Juan, San Salvador, El Salvador, 1980.

swallowing sight whole. They stand out against the dream-scenery. Their legs are not fragile looking at all, but well-proportioned like a Mission-style coffee table or Amish-made furniture. I am attracted to them implicitly. I approach them. They are poised at the edges of their webs most of the time. Sometimes they are off their webs but nearby. There is sometimes a kill on their webs. I approach them and see closer, feeling the fear a bit, but more the attraction. On their webs, there is a smaller brown spider near the kill. At first the brown spider looks like a completely different species. The possibility of them being the same kind of spider at different ages doesn't come to mind. It takes me a dream-minute to make the connection that perhaps this little brown spider is an offspring. A spider-child. The larger black spider is its caregiver. Its mother. It feeds the smaller brown spider.

When my grandparents died in 1978, when they were run over and left to die, I hadn't yet been conceived. My brother must have been a few months old. My brother started speaking at ten months. He knew the names of the bread man, the priest down the street, spoke in almost full sentences, and anticipated my arrival into this world, telling whomever he could that I was coming. This must have been uniquely exhausting for my parents, I first think. But then remember that my brother's family was much larger than mine. Grandparents visited him, bathed him, fed him, sat him on tractors and made diesel noises, spoke to him, read to him. Family was a short walk away, a quick drive in the car. His was a vibrant holding environment. He and I would be born into different worlds. My mother left her job after I was born. She had by then lost her parents. Her brothers had fled El Salvador. There was a war going on. I bring this up because it's important to recognize that she straddled distinct environmental realities and tried to make sense of the unique demands each reality made on her while caring for her children as a project so heavily engrossed in time as a speed. So heavy it brings cubital tunnel syndrome like acid rain on forearms. The quickness of a nap takes up an entire day. The duration of a cry stretches an instant into some spiraling, escalating abyss. The incrementality of growth and maturation deranges our collective sense of distance to horizons like independence. Day upon day. Yesterday like today. Tomorrow like yesterday. The feeling that there is no help coming. No one visiting for dinner. That *you* have to make this dinner that your parents will not taste. That dinner will last as long as it lasts, as long as the haunting silhouette of negative space in the shape of grandparents cooing and singing, despite not being able to share this food you will produce from a sudden and radical absence as if by magic itself.

    What I'm getting at is depression. But depression is a diagnosis, and I'm not qualified. Depression reminds one of this incredible ability to experience sensation. Perception, as the anticipation of the body's response to environment, is in a glitch of sorts. Ingurgitated by flood. Desiccated by drought. What I've been trying to engage with are ambient processes poetry frames as simultaneously scientific and affective responses, and by that I refer to the demonstrations of the soma that cannot be traced to any one genetic predisposition but rather to a network of possible environmental factors that make up life. Soma and retention. Language and experience. Bodies and evidence. Anger is an active verb that describes a process of cascading signals and shuttling ideas between felt parts of the body and the brain. Anger is also a form of address. And as an address there is a responsibility to sit with the discomfort of anger in the midst of competing states that offer other forms of relational potential, like love, like care, like affirmation. Anger is a necessary expression of perceived time in a culture's ability to adapt to place.

The poets I read in this final chapter are all of them female poets writing somatically. They write about gestation as a temporal dimension through which the world is interpreted in its being unkind, uncertain, its being a site of potentiation, futurity, and pessimism. But it is also about where the personal and public meet, that is, about poetry and politics. This meeting is a shared site of information at a fundamental register of soma and cognition. It's a touching of information where the facticity of event is a communal opportunity to develop a sense of care. Transgenerational injury is less about labeling somatic cellular adaptations between bodies that kind of look alike and maybe more about an environment that keeps replicating permissible injury, sanctioned necropolitics, and rationalized injury as a mode of governance inflicted onto bodies that share continuity. If governance is a way of thinking about relationality under the atmosphere of rules and guidelines regarding how to relate justly, then we must ask why we permit injurious and unjust relationships. We do so because these relationships operationalize what our bodies are capable of toward financing a historical narrative of exceptionalism. We permit some relationships to operationalize injury and pain as a way of ruling over bodies in the service of founding white-body principles: capitalism, order, nationalism, supremacy.

•••

When I consider my mother's different worlds, my initial desire is to locate myself in them to prove the existence of trauma within my very cells. But that seems to get it wrong, or at least there's a missed opportunity to make something out of it from the same viral situation of lived experience, and the "affective contagion" that cárdenas maps aesthetically. It seems more validating and fascinating to consider how what was present in my mother's worlds forms the challenges present in mine, despite the distance between El Salvador and the US, and how adaptation is the carrying out of generational confrontation with these challenges as structural reincarnations and reenactments of traumatizing worlding. In this disclosure, I think of Alexander's poetic speaker and the strength imparted by the everyday when it is magnified by poetics, which fits the disparate pieces of experience together as a whole existence. It is one that the societal influence of structural history attempts to partition into seemingly random, objective occurrences without intent. As I argue earlier, there is a distinction between true stochastic experience and colonialism. Stochastic events are random events. Colonialism's total grasp of the natural, spiritual, and political world since enveloping the hemisphere has sought to coopt felt stochastic probability toward blanketing the world-as-event in its own probability, its own logic.

Divya Victor's *CURB* is a counterintuitive to the probability of violence within the democratic national territory that is America. It is a docupoetic archive of witnessed spatiotemporality as a body of culture in America making sense of societal relationality at the same moment of spatial residency amidst violence and the colonial stretch of systemically valuing bodies according to white-body supremacy. This evaluation is not just the assimilative pressure of acceptance through mimesis, but also the necropolitical parallel to assimilation, which is death. A literal erasure of the spatial probability of public difference, and a worlding organized by culturally permissible (in fact structural) death. The book takes shape around four South Asian men who came to America only to die in America through acts of racial violence, and this experience is mitigated through the poet's body as a woman of culture in a generational relationship to family and distance, and as a pregnant woman of culture in a gestational relationship to her nervous system and the flashes of nervous development of the fetus.

> My father likes to say: *how far we have come.* My mother likes to say: *how long it has been.* I want a body that answers these questions together, knowing fully that these are not questions but statements about having arrived, somewhere, alone together.[6]

This line resonates with me, "arrived somewhere alone, together." It describes every photo I've ever seen of my family during our first decade in America and the experience of being marked "immigrant" in America. I can put myself in Victor's poetics. My mother wondering "how long it has been" since she last touched her parents. My father "how far we have come" from the scene of their deaths, an aftermath he had to see firsthand. I measure my children's ages in the length of time since my parents last saw them. I measure my age in how far I've come from the lunarscape places in the photos of my childhood. We lived, it seems, everywhere no one really wanted to live,

dreams

FIGURE 16. Here, nowhere, together, Salt Lake, Utah, 1980 something.

eastern California, southern Arizona, central Utah. My relationship to my own soma, I realize when reading Victor, can be described by the panic over a body "knowing fully" the condition of Being in America. Our sense of the ontological is a perception rattling between a history I've not had much say in and a migration I've not had much say in, and the felt attachments that condition my sensory availability to feel settled. I also "want a body that answers" the questions in front of me. I suspect, however, that the desire in Victor's lyric is more closely attuned to the desire in cárdenas's speaker, and her gestational awareness of the multitudes inside her. I wonder how this level of somatically aware nerve-mapping informs a person's ability to exist with others in the recognition of a cultural adaptation against the societal influences of binary living, of publics organized by assimilation and erasure.

It says something about migrants that we are keener to keep a record of changes in a cultural, not societal sense, because movement and change present challenges that must be met even when—and they most often are—unsettling and uncomfortable. Even when they present challenges to the physics of perception itself, when they braid the axes of space and time yet remain asymptotic, never crossing over. I am referring to "culture" in the evolutionary sense of a human awareness of learning how to live, not mimesis, that is, the ensouled sense of Menakem's abolitionist practices of liberating bodies, plural, from the hold of mimetic "social acceptance" toward a reorientation of true, hormonal contentment from the work of belonging. Every adaptation in a diaspora is in response to a direct challenge for which there is little precedent recorded in shared publics, as archives, for what to do, how to imitate. We are armed with repertoires, which Diana Taylor describes as "non archival system[s] of transfer" through which performance "persists," which is to say, refuses erasure.[7] Poetry extends these movements and attunements, especially experimental poetics with their performative, postlyric elements. We know, instinctually, that assimilation is not adaptation, because the public performances of assimilation disappear into the dominant and enforced roles. They disappear, in fact, into enforcement as compliance. It is a violence we internalize, and yet know it is not cultural. When we are "alone together," however, we engage in simultaneous forms of reassurance. The immediateness of need is recognized to be hormonal and the mitigated contemplative panic over assuredness in the political sense of what we fight for in our frustrated demands to be seen, not spectacularized. We fight internally against societal influence and how it disfigures.

"I realize that in these pills there is a home for me," writes cárdenas in "Pregnancy," a clinging to life in an atmosphere of genocide.

> these pills, and all the changes they've brought to my body and life,
> have brought me to a place of commitment to building a home and
>   a family, to heal the deepest wounds in myself,
> to care for myself and those I love,
> by creating stability,
> by being careful with our hearts and our lives.
> Funny that my Colombian father's whole way of raising me,
> was to teach me to be the man, the breadwinner,
> and it didn't work at all,
> but absolutely rejecting man in the deepest way I could
> brought me full circle to want to create and protect my family,
> in a way that dad
> will one day appreciate.[8]

If I think of cárdenas and Victor solely within the question of genre, there is still a lot to gain as far as a cultural imaginary and a working awareness of

American publics. "Genre exists in no small part to smooth over antagonisms and conflicts," writes Travis M. Foster, "to reattach us... and to help us feel a sense of connection to the conventions that enable shared experience. It mediates the *we* and maps out belonging within it."[9] There is nothing radical to the evolution of genre in an analysis that animates the existence of anger or negative affect, experimentalism, or identity-centered approaches to parsing lyric voice. The radicality is in the shift in attention between expected "conventions" to expected "shared experiences," or put differently, the realization that the experiences of lyric speakers exhibiting critical reproach of the status quo are themselves part of the milieu wherein the status quo is experienced as the everyday. Analysis of this sort "enables analysis of the significance and complexity of conventions while also facilitating understanding of the relationship between those conventions and the departures from them."[10]

The poetry I've been focusing on departs from exceptionalist displays of beneficent and benevolent publics and often refutes the principles of a "good" democratic public. Maybe this poetry can be experienced as an injury or as injurious. A morete is a bruise, an echo of tissue trauma and evidence of susceptibility. They can be deeply purple, or purplish, because they never stay the same hue. The double consciousness of "purplish" opens the performative moral bond between the PR campaign of complicit white nationalism throughout the Midwest and health, revealing the difference between tissue trauma and the moralistic abstraction of historical exceptionalism through a cellular measure of damage. I'm a neurotic observer of my body. This makes me a neurotic observer of my body's surroundings as well. I am aware of all the processes deemed excess from economized calculations of what my body is worth and of how it's meant to contribute to a "good" society. Poetry helps us understand the simultaneity of being embodied by experience and being disembodied through the power of hurtful ideas. While individuals are permitted personal displays of joy, anger is always interrogated. It must be proven. It resonates with calls for testimony, evidence, corroboration. And this book celebrates poetry that archives the evidence of discomfort.

When Rawls theorizes a body politic organized around a genetic benevolence he is relying on interrelation as an implicit principle of human cohabitation. But he is not honestly making a study of the materialist archives of relationality in the Americas, which must include all the darkness and edges through and against which bodies have come into relationship with one another and learned, even, how they must relate to themselves via a social value to be loved. Rawls is relying on beneficence. What I am talking about is exploitation, necropolitics, and racial supremacy through eugenic assumptions that pass in our cultural consciousness as epistemology. We are asymptotic, not crisscrossing tissue—the perverse metaphor of benevolent relation on which Rawls premises beneficence as the violent realities of colonialism.

I think about my mother being pregnant with me because I wasn't conscious at that time, but *this* primitive nervous system in-development, *my* nervous system, was in a direct and understudied relationship with the vagal network through which she processed the loss of her parents, war, and the shock of migration. We were linked in the rather unique way of pure adaptation without societal evaluation and yet insisted upon by societal influences as much as environmental ones. Our experience as a family has always been one of radical intimacy. I can't imagine a version of our lives not organized around the system of family I experienced growing up. I have to believe that this radicality originates in the somatic consciousness mapped early in these events. I have realized while doing my own work that clearly both my parents experience the world through bodies that existed in the world, coming to terms with stress and trauma in their own way. There is a chain of care I carry over into my relationship with my family, the family I live with predominantly: my spouse, my children. It flows in our house like butter when my parents visit and my kids wake up shiny with it, their curls matted and smelling of it.

Adrenaline is called the emergency hormone because it causes dilation of the blood vessels in response to a sudden and powerful expenditure. When I read micha cárdenas I can almost hear this like tinnitus. When I read Victor's poetics of gestation I feel the tinnitus in the language marking stone steps, "milestones" of movement.

> Every migrant body should keep company with its living
> Milestones. To mark another day when it has roamed, without
> Extinguishing itself on the fire of a crossing or being bludgeoned
> Into forgetfulness or threatened into monolingualism.
>
> A mark in the body to remember the work of being discard.
>
> A mark in the body to remember the work of being *itinerant-latecomer-belated-party crasher-imposter-undocumented-*

stranger danger-trespasser-terrorist-gorgeous eyes-wherefromfrom-fresh off the boat-pretty hair-great asset-no Offense takener-international talent-sorry to butcher your Name-tax burden-welfare monster-visa monger-anchor babe-Migrant-kith.[11]

Yes, I am still talking about my mother's depression, even while I think about poetry that engages with broader experiences. I'm not, however, wanting to equate injury to injury, or to spectacularize pain, reduce everything down to a glowing sheen of adrenaline sweat on a shivering body propped onto the stage, under the lights. These injuries exist in a timespace. Exist as it, in fact, as far as our sensations go. What I wonder is if our repertoires are forced into archiving pain in place of ceremony. I am sensitive to intergenerational stress because I have lived with a deep, clinical sensation of depression that I realized recently is more accurately a sensation of loss—both past loss and the prediction of loss. I am not a body permitted to grieve, however, without upsetting those who mourn the loss of their positional superiority when equity upsets the status quo. These are intimate affinities, and maybe that's why it's never been a question for me that anger is an important sentient demonstration that a public cannot be a public without.

When Victor writes "a mark in the body" there is a literalness to it. Her practice involves a lot of somatic performance during composition. She puts her body in a locale; she orients her body to cardinal points as well as to specific coordinates mapping familial memory and transnational journeys, to water, to home, to people. She describes the sensation of her body in this practice of orientation and reorientation. The poetry picks up on this literal sensation, which is what I mean by "intimacy" in a lyric sense. I want to be cautious in concluding that this is a somaticization of address itself, because we should be cautious of somaticizing anything that is not of the body. But there is a translation of sensation that heightens language in a manner that supplants the hold rhetoric has in the social function of speaking. Such that, what intimacy and performance accomplish, especially when articulated through bodies that are "marked" in publics, is the realization of a third language, so to speak. This language is one capable of observing diaspora, fugitivity, and the idioms of "discard" and attuned toward justice.

The coordinates of dead Southeast Asian men on American sidewalks are an intentional making of a lyric haunt in each utterance throughout the book. "This book was made to witness the following irreducible facts," Victor writes in her book's dedication, continuing, "these men once lived; they loved; they were loved. The United States of America is responsible for the force of feeling and action that ended their lives."

Of particular interest is the somatic-gestational documentation of the poetic speaker's sensation of "fact," as news regarding anti-Asian violence. It is so utterly felt as an abomination of global democratic modernity that fetal nervous systems cling to and confer with the uterine nervous system in attempting to preserve an essential, reparative bond of communication, transmission, resistance, and worlding.

> When I read the news
> of the shooting, this belly
> plumed into an apse.[12]

Victor writes this in "THRESHOLD." An apse is an architectural space for the alter at one end, often the eastern end, of a house of worship. But it's the "this" and "this here" we pay attention to. A pointing-at that is documenting sensation, orienting the nervous response synching to the nervous development of the fetus toward and away from violence.

> — it distended
> upward, a balloon hollow
> but leaden, these lungs lifted
> here — this diaphragm fled, bore through
> a tent made of ligament
> & rope.
>
> ... Here — this belly
> carrying those pounds of flesh
> began to take flight[13]

The news is the news of Srinivas Kuchibhotla being shot by a white supremacist in Kansas. The haunt is a death that hops from one body, resembling in this case her father's, to the next. But the vagus is the soul nerve, as Menakem calls it. It is a uniquely ancient sort of communicative power to name and be named, settled and settle.

When I read the news, the she in me
was swollen & pressing, & I saw
her dropping to kneel, her
brown belly
collapsed to a city's curb
her skull crimson in the clouds
her sweet ear flung & clinging
to a parapet.

... I looked
within this — here — belly
for those eyes that could tell
dark apart from light, & I wished
out loud
so she could survive —
     live, I said,
     in any skin, live.[14]

This insistence of "here," and "this here," is a provocative kind of apostrophe in that in its occupying also the function of address orients the sensory circuitry between speaker and nervous system, as well as reader, to event. If not in a direct manner of optic reference, these are spatial cues graphed onto the form of the human body. The optic cueing is overshadowed by the sensation of the performance and the poet's transmission of the feeling, which although hyperspecific and synced to her gestational-spatiotemporal awareness, and even though within the bigger spatiotemporal kairos of a diaspora landed in the violence of America, arrives to us, the audience, as a transcendent call to care for survival via an awareness of constituent parts of the whole organ of the body. Indeed, the worldmaking power of this work is in how care is turned into a universal sensation of poetic meaning and poetic idiom. Care is a reanimated conclusion from flesh that is not cared for, except in those who share the inevitable vulnerability of being rendered a similar kind of flesh, marked as "discard." It is flesh portrayed as receptive to violent stimulation, but not recognized for its eloquence to utter in response to that aroused somatic-adaptive performativity, especially that arousal toward an adaptive cultural transformation. This poetry is that response. And in it, this poetry includes the memories and testimony of every single body of flesh that swells, and presses, and distends toward any available apse wherein its utterance might be carried over and amplified by the structure and form of the sacred and intentional design of the dome and assembled therein.

• • •

> Dearest, living is beneath you. infested as it is by our nostalgic narratives of hope. here exists for itself alone. as your form passes through. stay your soul in mine. keep your room. my womb. as hermitage. these hours now are ours.[15]

Claudia Rankine also has a somatic-gestational poetics in the form of *Plot*, published years before the work that would attune peoples' attention to American exceptionalism like *Citizen* and *Just Us*. I would argue *Plot* was doing this already, but with an intimacy that readers were unwilling to grasp without some sort of social bearing that would permit the majority of them to ignore the implications of adaptation even while engaging with a social justice discourse. The intimacy of a pessimism as gestational address is perhaps too much for the religio-secular historicity of "life" in America, as well as its being racialized between white and Black mothers, and the dignity of sentience parceled out to each according to the value of their children in a long logic of operationalization.

I do wonder if there are any photos of my mother while pregnant with me because we would be in El Salvador, not America, and it would be the only visual evidence of my primitive nervous system contracting and shouting, spreading, and settling as non-American. But, I've never seen any and so I've never asked. There is only one photo I know of my mother between my brother's birth and mine, and it's lost forever. It's a photo of my family, the family I would become part of, at the beach. The beach is called El Majahual. I've driven through it now as an adult several times, but I've never pulled over. My grandfather, my mother's father, is said to have taken the photo. My mother is standing at the surf's edge holding my brother in her arms. I've used this photo in different projects, often sketching it while I work. I made an etching of it ages ago. The image is part of a ritual, one that involves sensing my way through remnant traces of an original language (a third language). It's inconceivable to me that my parents would have another child when they did. They are radical people. They are and have always been avant-garde. I understand the historical context frozen into the sepia breath brushed over the photo to have been an ambient turbulence raucously demanding attention outside the frame of what is captured. I wonder about the existential tug of war she must have engaged in, maybe similar to Liv's, the poetic speaker in *Plot*, in weighing the societal moralization of a biological process she would not have much control over. Birth, miscarriage, keeping a fetal grapefruit inside through the extending branches of vagal intention. Especially given my mother had a traumatic miscarriage before my brother's birth. Especially given the sudden loss of her parents on an otherwise banal evening in San Salvador, after dinner.

The momentum of gestation is a process that occupies time in a way that moves consciousness toward a bifurcation, toward a difference reconciled. Victor calls this a kind of twinning. Ruminating on post-gestational time for many children in America, Rankine writes, "Dearest, living is beneath you." If it were to be only mere living, societal in the relationships that occupy living, the "hope" and the disillusionment are all part of an operationalized extraction. To "exist for" existence alone is a rather different call, and I say call because it requires a "here." Gestation is not the dimensionless space of a vacuum. The microscope cárdenas uses reveals the activity of dimension and process undergirding daily life.

How does one say "what if" without "reproach," without distortion? This rhetorical game seems exhausting. It's maybe this exhaustion, however, that ignites the soma. There is something to being exhausted by poetry that leaves us in a better state than where we started, when we started.

I don't want to bestow on my fetal-self angel wings or anything of the sort, but I imagine a moment like Liv's taking place in my mother's body, a soft symphony of tinnitus landing like light on the realization that "here exists for itself alone." Then the arrival of time in moments that she finds herself each instant more clarified in, more resolute, moving, expanding. My mother carried her abdomen into gestation like evolution in a tar pit. I like to believe my "soul stayed" with hers, that when she feels an anger or a hope it comes from a sensation that we both share, even if the frequency has been lost over time of static distraction. I like to feel that I have a bit of her magic when I touch my children's hair, convinced as I am that my mother has always been able to read my mind. Because why shouldn't she be able to? She put it together like a beaver mushes together its mud chapel. Her body pressed and expanded, fitted together, transported charges from here to there, to "here."

I am sensitive to this sensation because I was conditioned at an early age through my relationship to my family, and my family was at the time of my early childhood destabilized by specific events that then flavored our general atmosphere as immigrants. We prepared for depression through expressions of love and fear, through allegiances and ambivalence. We prepared for joy through injury, and intentional naming of the violator as if to say: No. We will not internalize *your* weakness. We prepared under a dome of sky and photographed ourselves doing so. I do think my own poetry is an attempt to do the same, capture the scene of our bodies in this space. We are captured, prepared in the ballistic relationships equally frozen in a chemical print, ¡chicharros!

My adrenaline is a hormonal wave the current of which is pulled by euphoria as a temporal dimension on the other side of a first impression. What I like about dreams, even what some would consider to be nightmares, is how the thin membrane between conceptual time and experiential time is made even thinner by the confusing state of narrative arousal. Conceptual time is a flow of time: past, present, future. Experiential time is somatic. It is dominated by the emergence of now. Dream time is not the same as gestational time, which is where I've been moving in this last chapter. But I also don't have a gestational awareness as a nonuterine body. I have the power of memory as a terrain to explore, which makes mine a clumsy body in this thinking about intergenerational affect and its national relationship to genre. I focus on the gestating body because the period marked by gestation as the awareness of development, contingent on the primary health of one's "host" body, makes for a marked awareness of vulnerability to passing adaptations or triggering adaptations through the body as a membrane to the environment.

The approaching of these two temporal dimensions animated within gestational-somatic poetics brings together the two equally different states of awareness operative in each. Where we've arrived at is an adaptive responsiveness to our very plasticity. A collective self-awareness and acceptance of change in the totalizing sense of revolution that mere "progress" or "progressive change" doesn't seem able to accomplish. We've arrived at a euphoria in the awareness of survival as a collective act. Not because "progress" as such is dysfunctional. Some might say it is. I'm not interested in litigating progressiveness. To me progressiveness exists within a discursive tension that has been torqued by after-colonial colonialism in the first place. I am interested in liberation. I am interested in foregrounding, celebrating, and charting the euphoria of survival. Because what we call progress is a homeostatic system of knowledge, not as the verification of exceptionalism, but its absurdity in an utter non-existent importance when it comes to adaptive change, or life. Progress is the survival that can be happening right now, in the present, as a species.

I keep these photos of my family because of what they whisper to me about group survival. This is what diaspora can be about. Over the last few years, I've become obsessed with and ambivalent toward what is often called transgenerational trauma in a psychiatric or therapeutic sense. There is a lot of potential for bodies to explore their memories, and transgenerational trauma has been key for families making sense of their ancestral relationship to and through the Holocaust. But I also understand that most likely nothing happened at a somatic-cellular level between my mother's uterus and me, a developing fetus. I don't know that for sure, obviously, and there are studies that support the idea of adaptive processes in times of metabolic stress, in particular.[16]

I am more and more convinced by cellular biologists on the question of epigenetic adaptation in this context of trauma. I would never discount it as an organizing sense of time for bodies engaged in processing pain. But it is clear to me that as a group we run close to a dangerous assumption regarding healing in this context that transliterates nineteenth-century perspectives on individual deficit and the exceptionalism of eugenic Reason. Trauma, getting back to Resmaa Manekem, is a framework for understanding response, reflex, and retention, and thus a framework for response-time and reflexive patterns as cascading information between somatic and neurological signals that pattern our habits of behavior as they function alongside the prediction making organ of the brain. This is about worldmaking. It is historical in the sense of how generations of marked bodies spark a similar charge of difference in a white-body society, against a white-body standard, of how those bodies are integrated into white-body exceptionalisms in a way that is threatening, disqualifying, and systemic. Transgenerational white-body exceptionalism emerges in the sense of eliciting a choice, a decision on association, not just as social survival but hormonally as the stress of belonging, mattering, and safety.

I keep photos of my family because they nourish my response-sensitivity. I am an archivist of time-stamps, of the affective. A lot of my thinking revolves around perspectives on epigenetics from different disciplinary demands on epigenetics as an explanatory science for time-stamping. First, I must establish some parameters. I don't think the body is, itself, an archive of experiences. The body is an instrument the brain plays through pressure and breath, electricity, and anticipatory reflexes. Many therapeutic discourses center the soma as a site for patients to focus on, and though I don't believe the body keeps the score, so to speak, I do believe the body can serve a more active role in rewriting the brain's narratives through which it perceives and anticipates the world.

Epigenetics has offered a radical framework for thinking about intergenerational experiences with similarly shaped traumatic injuries, especially injuries provoked societally. Cellular alignment, however, locates injury within a somatic narrative containing the temporal possibility of my mother as a dilated image of time that also includes the ways my possibilities might appear in moments of reflection. An epigenetic framework, in other words, grants an intimate space amidst flux, change, and adaptation. Part of me is hesitant to grant this. I want sentience. I want an after-colonial revolution of the sensible as a framework of justice, not just the public display of the intimate for the entertainment of the audience. And I want sentience to be as public as a Civil War monument, as public as the neighborhood bar, as a Carvana vending machine seen from the freeway. Our adaptations will come from the rewriting of discomfort as address. To inherit injury is altogether something else. What I realize is also present between the worlds my mother has negotiated, and the environments I have found to be most inhospitable to my body are shared circumstances that organize my actual freedom and the freedom of other bodies like mine within a spectrum of differences that signal "non-white-body" under the exceptionalism of white-body supremacy. On one hand, the familial intimacy of diaspora trauma as inherited trauma gives "us" power, but on the other, it alienates "us" from a bigger assembly of others bracing themselves as smaller emotional units and family systems.

It would take years for me to learn that nervous arousal could be transformed into conscious action, or that discomfort is an astute awareness of complexity, or how every single bump of flexed skin on my arm is an orientation of how each goosebump points its head toward collective frequencies as if to scream, ¡vecinos! in goosebump speak, or ¡chicharros! in a more universal grammar of attention. When I think about my own work, my "genre agnosticism," as my friend Doug so beautifully describes it,[17] I reflect on a deep investment in the agency and sentience of transformation to begin in a circuitry of legible experience. But it must move into arrangements that heighten this almost cellular awareness to environmental events as evidence of an observable reality around which publics coalesce, ready to validate, confront, challenge, or revise culture. Not doing so makes a spectacle of the lyric's power to summon its people. Politics may be about conflicts over meaning, which I think is Chantal Mouffe's biggest critique of Rawls, when she writes that the "problematic implications for a pluralist approach" rest in "his conception of a 'well-ordered society,'" and that "one of its main shortcomings is precisely that it tends to erase the very place of the adversary, thereby expelling any legitimate opposition from the democratic public sphere."[18] Agonistic parties also recognize a truth in observability and respect sentience as a human dignity that braids our bodies to place and amplifies our voice through the temporality of expression as a form of relationality that is not premised on operationalized spectacularization.

Poetry gives form to all the possible combinations and codes the brain might dispatch toward moving the body through space and in time with their environments, which include the choreography of others, and often shared stimuli, shared desires, shared predictions, or shared outcomes: assembly, in other words. Poetry gives shape to the circumstances of assembly from the human perspective of feelings, which are themselves the copies of "ideations" for action, movement, and survival—sensation, in other words—and as the scientist Lisa Feldman Barrett so clearly articulates it in *How Emotions Are Made*, what are actually "perceptions": "An emotion is your brain's creation," argues Barrett, "of what your bodily sensations mean, in relation to what is going on around you in the world."[19] In other words, we don't uniquely experience the sensory information that comes in through our bodies; we construct "feelings" from history and predictive adaptations, which is to say, from context. I would add that poetic emotions signal this environmental context, and it is both transparently historical and political and performative of an immunology, marking a body's prolonged exposure and adaptation to stress and repair. Our brains interpret the environment subperceptibly and continuously. What we refer to as "sensations," especially in the moment of feeling them, are in fact "perceptions" that our brain, through sensory inputs, have already made sense of through past experiences, that is, memory. I wonder, as a nonscientist, if there exists in my vagal circuitry a memory of being stimulated by my mother's response to unwelcome change in her life. Poetry, in giving shape to circumstances for human spatiotemporality, or worlding, accomplishes form in the same dimensional ways as this. Language, as a discernment, has made sense of experiences already, and yet our embodiment comes to events that trigger this nervous-cognitive cascade. What poetry does that is of course more dimensional, is that it gives form to the perceptible as well as the subperceptible. It discloses this mystery in a way that offers audience a prophetic dilation within which to adapt to confrontation and paradox, particularly without having to rely purely on societal instinct.

• • •

Anger is an action that moves bodies across their conclusions in the service of a desired outcome. I may be attending to depression, but the socially aware arousal that matters often starts as the sensation of anger. Anger can move into the drop in space we feel as loss. It starts in a moment of anger at the world experienced by my mother in San Salvador the moment her parents were taken from her child, and from her life, by an organization that was also uninterested in how this loss would affect her forever. She was not a real person to the officers at the US Embassy whom she and my father and my uncles reproached in their search for justice. And yet, there we were a year later touching down in America. The patterns and influences I am describing are not unique to my family. Many have experienced similar culturally formative events.

A world full of war and uncertainty blasted a jagged hole in the papier mâché horizon, and my parents gathered what they could and walked through it into America. Photos of snowy landscapes and grayish looking lakes. Donated puffy coats and weird hats. The kinds of generic uncomfortable kid's shoes that make me cry whenever I think of them. They left behind unsettled ghosts and two gravesites we wouldn't be able to return to or put flowers on for nearly thirteen years.

My father, I am learning more and more as I grow older, cannot live without my mother. While the story of my maternal grandparents occupies the greater part of my young memory, as an emotional unit my father's decision-making in the face of change and circumstance is worth noting in my attention to the empowering experiences of anger in the face of instability and contradiction. Most studies that explore paternal transmission of gene alleles effected by increases in cortisol are conducted with mice. And yet I can't deny the taste of butter in my mouth when I am around my dad in times of stress. We're not mice, but "how far we've come" seems to be an innate code he and I share, as much as "how long it has been" is one I share with my mother. The ghost sensation of butter as a unit of space in our mouths is not societal in influence, but a taste learned through experimentation. When I walked around Los Angeles eating free pupusas, how many sidewalks did I share with the ghostly steps of my father, who at fifteen ran away from home and with a friend bought a Mercury and drove to Los Angeles, where he lived for a few years working at a Unical 76 and learning English at night? How far did we walk the same stretch up and down Vermont, Melrose, Sunset? The taste is language like fat on our palates, distance like stomach pain measured in duration.

But epigenetics is a tricky subject.

How can I believe in wandering souls and transmitted pain? I believe this because it's a survival strategy in the face of our specific colonial inheritance of a public sphere where only ancestral ghostly haunts are permitted equal access to politics. Writing in *Just Us* Claudia Rankine analyzes the spatial history of white privilege in "assumptions of privilege and exclusion that have led many white Americans to call the police on Black people trying to enter their own homes or vehicles. Racial profiling becomes another sanctioned method of segregating space."[20] Spatial segregation via expectations carried out in profiling includes dispositional assessments of non-white bodies in predominantly white-body spaces, reflected in this passage from a police report describing a racial profiling incident:

> **He seemed angry and swore at me, stating that he was an employee at the university. I realized at this time that my body camera was not on and I reached down and opened the shutter. He unlocked the door to this residence and began walking inside. I again stated that I just wanted to explain why I was stopping him and asked if he would talk to me. He then slammed the door and remained inside. I walked away from the residence and back to my squad car.**
> CN: #▓▓▓▓, 9/26/2016. Officer: 602 – ▓▓▓▓▓▓▓

Police report: my purple neighborhood. Eau Claire, Wisconsin, 2016.

If I am to believe in environmental beneficence, then it's only non-embodied versions of difference that may coexist with dominant definitions of social actors. Actors capable of imposing societal influence on par with dominant influences, like capital. Poetry offers a different relational paradigm to sociality, which is culture. Poetry is a radical form of the written record that portrays an adaptive potential from relationships that describe culture. This probably explains why so much early humanist writing consistently equated race to environment, attempting to monopolize habitat adaptability and moralize violence as part of that adaptive drive. But this is not fundamentally the same linguistic event of cultural evolution. Colonialism premised its authority on social influence. On public burnings. On lynching. On eugenics.

Culture is not any one thing. We are currently living through what can be argued to be a maladaptive phase premised on homogeneity as a shortcut to environmental stability. This is what DinéYazhí describes as the postapocalyptic tendency to replace creation with colonialism. The imbalance that is a purple societal code of behavior is based more on the instinct to preserve colonialism than on cultural adaptation, or cultural evolution. Colonialism is a social instinct transformed into governance, moral code, legal systems. It found its way into the patterns and rhythms of life, aesthetics, and generic narratives amidst the public reaffirming instinct over difference. This anger that I've been carrying through this book is not instinct. It is a harnessing of hormonal swell.

But back to those spiders.

If I am to decode these dream-messages, I suppose the reading that makes the most sense to me, and who I am right now, is that these spiders are mother spiders. My androgenic-nonuterine biases aside, what this means to me is an intimacy through which to study environment and time, arousal and adaptation. Intragenerational twins, as Victor describes the feeling, is maybe another way to describe how our nervous systems share an environmental reality. The web they exist on and rely on as they pass down their knowledge to their spider-children is an implicitly strong one, yet it is delicate in the context of how I look at them from a position that is not contingent on their survival for my survival. There is a differential, in other words. A dilation of positionality that translates into the awareness of survival as a shared experience. I recognize the potential of making an imprint by stimulating the web. Phenomenally, would they respond to my impulsive violence, or would they retain the stress, respond to the stress? Earlier I made the claim that I don't think my cellular self is methylated in any significant way. Dilation spreads stimuli like a jam, that kind of invisible layer of sugar that gets on everything. I didn't have to inherit cellular adaptation in utero because I experienced the same violent world via an intimate vagal circuit. America is indeed an intimate address.

• • •

notes

introduction: ¡chicharros!

1. Menakem, *My Grandmother's Hands*, 5.
2. See Moten, *Stolen Life*, 266–67.
3. As Muñoz puts it, "Brownness is a kind of uncanny persistence in the face of distressed conditions of possibility." See *Sense of Brown*, 4.
4. Foster, *Genre and White Supremacy*, 14.
5. Culler, "Lyric, History, and Genre," 886.
6. I'm thinking here of the work by Dr. Robert Malenka and his laboratory. Much of this new modeling comes from studying the brain's reward circuitry, and Dr. Malenka's foundational work in this area stems from examining addiction and the brain's plasticity under addictive patterning. See, for example, Walsh, Christoffel, and Malenka, "Neural Circuits Regulating Prosocial Behaviors."
7. Menakem connects modern forms of torture to medieval and early modern European public executions by means of drawing and quartering and to the less historically distant practice of lynching. He does this to include white bodies in the need for somatic abolitionism, arguing that white bodies arrived in the Americas retaining trauma from having witnessed acts of public, national violence. See *My Grandmother's Hands*, 202–4.
8. An imaginary critiqued often by thinkers from Chantal Mouffe and Wendy Brown to Fred Moten, Sara Ahmed, and Calvin Warren.
9. The cartogram in figure 1 is by Mark Newman, based on county-by-county data from the 2016 presidential election. Maps and cartograms are licensed under Creative Commons and are free to use. For more on Newman's work, see https://public.websites.umich.edu/~mejn/election/2016/.
10. Jadhav, "Was It Rural Populism?," 553.
11. Much of my analysis of democratism is grounded in Rawlsian concepts of the good or benevolence, justice and morality, and the "mutuality . . . implicit in the principles of justice," which I trace back to Reconstruction-era white-body supremacy (see Rawls, *A Theory of Justice*, chapter 8, "The Sense of Justice"). My analysis, moreover, is carried out in the context of my personal viewpoint on living through the political temporalities correlated to somatic-cognitive health

and on that health being a variable in a correlational matrix that brings practices and institutions of justice into the light of embodied experience.
12. Rawls, 438.
13. Lezra, *Defective Institutions*, 200.
14. Scully, *Democratic Anarchy*, 26.
15. Jadhav, 556.
16. Wells, "The New Cry," "Southern Horrors" (1892), n.p.
17. Harney and Moten, *The Undercommons*, 98.
18. See *Estéticas decoloniales,* Pedro Pablo Gómez Moreno and Walter Mignolo, 14. I refer to Mignolo because *aesthesis* is aimed at Global North aesthetics and my critique is of Global North exceptionalism. This is not, much like the arcane electoral maps, a clear binary map of hemisphere, as Global North exceptionalism operates in the southernmost regions of hemisphere. Exceptionalism is a multiscalar geography of power. Moreover, some of Mignolo's thinking is very clearly praxis, not concept or theory, and this is what I am relying on in my thinking about the poetry.
19. Menakem, 246.
20. Richerson and Boyd, *Not by Genes Alone*, 100.
21. See George Washington Cable, *The Negro Question* (1903), 43–46.
22. See, for instance, Said (1975), *Beginnings*, xvi.
23. My marriage counselor reminded me once of Brené Brown's work on resentment as being of the envy, not the anger, family of emotions.
24. Menakem, 205.
25. See Ignacio Martín-Baró, "Political Violence and War as Causes of Psychological Trauma in El Salvador," *International Journal of Mental Health* 18 (1): 3–20; and "War and the Psychological Trauma in Salvadoran Children," in *Writings for a Liberation Psychology*, 122–35.

soma

1. Menakem, 138.
2. A reference to Kevin Hassett's May 25, 2020 CNN interview.
3. I think about that thin space between Nathan Phillips and Nick Sandmann. What's happening there? Between what is potentially a smirk, a smile, a song, a prayer, a fear, a grotesque delight? For those not familiar with the image, to me the debate following the photograph encapsulates the spatial freedom to feel under white-body supremacy and everyone else's dispositional, second-class citizenship to white-body feelings.
4. I'm thinking of Beatrice Adler-Bolton and Artie Vierkant's work in *Health Communism*: "The pervasive myth of the malingerer—whose infectious dependency will bring about certain doom—is supported by the alleged eugenic/fiscal burden threatened if the surplus class were allowed to grow unchecked" (43).

5. We are often taught to keep our desires separate from strategy or planning. I believe joy and planning are inseparable. Stefano Harney and Fred Moten's writing in *The Undercommons* has been liberatory for me, particularly in how they frame "the party" of what's going. Also liberatory are images and videos of queer demonstrations where demonstrators dance opposition and confrontation, the most notable being videos of the cast of *Heartstoppers*, a British television show, dancing in the face of counterdemonstrators during London Pride in March 2022.
6. Harney and Moten, 98.
7. Menakem, 137.
8. Chan, *Revenge of the Asian Woman*, 45.
9. Chan, 43.
10. Chan, 43.
11. Studies that rely on binary understandings of "healthy" or "unhealthy" bodies (BMI, "lean," "overweight," "depressed," "adjusted") result in inconclusive findings on what these signals in fact mean about the vagus nerve and eating. All I want to underscore is that there is a nervous communication between the "gut" and the brain, as Menakem frames it, and the paradox of futurity and epidemiology, as Muñoz does.
12. Chan, 49.
13. Chan, 52.
14. Chan, 79.
15. Muñoz, 121.
16. Muñoz, 123.
17. Chan, 55.
18. Muñoz, 121.
19. Muñoz, 123.
20. These lines are from "Butter," a poem on page 36 of Elizabeth Alexander's *Body of Life* (1996).
21. At the time I was writing this, Jason Aldean's "Try That in a Small Town" was receiving considerable publicity, an illustration of nostalgia as a racist dog whistle summoning others to commit violence.
22. Alexander, "Trayvon Generation," *New Yorker*.
23. Menakem, 139.
24. Joshua Nguyen interview with Gauri Awasthi, published in *Offing*, September 16, 2022.
25. The phrase, attributed to Porfirio Díaz, reads in Spanish, ¡Pobre Méjico! ¡Tan lejos de Dios y tan cerca de los Estados Unidos!
26. Culler, 886.
27. Nguyen, 17.
28. Menakem, 147.
29. See Walsh, Christoffel, and Malenka, "Neural Circuits Regulating Prosocial Behaviors."

30. Nguyen, "Q&A with Joshua Nguyen."
31. Menakem, 146.
32. To be fair, this training is often delivered as "modules" that fail to fully humanize the situations wherein people experience trauma. But the point that time is perceived as an interval of competing forms of activity valued according to neoliberal principles remains fundamental.

trauma

1. Angel Dominguez, *Desgraciado: The Collected Letters*, 27.
2. Lloyd Bitzer, "The Rhetorical Situation," 5.
3. This quotation is from a version of Hicok's essay published in the *Utne Reader* in 2019; the original publication appeared in the *Michigan Quarterly Review* in 2018.
4. Hicok, "The Promise of American Poetry—Utne."
5. Michael White frames chaos as the disjunctive reality patients exhibit when the "landscape of identity" is misaligned with the "landscape of action" from which their identities manifest as such. Chaos is the expression of a temporal schism, which we might also think about relationally, as in a body of color's relation to law, in the present, wherein law carries residues of the past (long past and near past); residues that are expressed at times when laws interact with said body or bodies like it in a public manner. This is maddening. See, for instance, White's *Maps of Narrative Practice*.
6. Dominguez, 55.
7. Bayesian statistics weighs both observable and unobservable probabilities equally and provides the statistical mode used in the neuroscientific understanding of interoceptive predictive signaling, namely, how the brain constantly makes adaptive predictions based on felt probability from past experiences, via the interoceptive signaling cascades that include, among other neural receptive sites, the amygdala. This understanding has upended the classic interpretation of the brain as a passive site activated only when responding to stimuli, rather than the active network of signals and predictive processing, which it actually is.
8. Dominguez, 27.
9. Ahmed, *Cultural Politics of Emotion* (2004 edition), 4.
10. Wynter, "Unsettling the Coloniality of Being/Power/Truth/Freedom," 306.
11. Dominguez, 15.
12. Dominguez, 24.
13. Carl Schmidt's twentieth-century differentiation between direct and indirect power has served as a model for institutional animation and the conceit of a political truth on the horizon line of institutional-power and its objectives. Much like Rawlsian morality, however, this is a dangerous underconsideration of dissensus. Political truth and direct power, or influence, can easily become a

euphemism for dominant and unwavering perspectives regarding "culture" and politics, or non-Christian moral "ideology," marking many of us outside politics.

14. See, for instance, H. D. Critchley and N. A. Harrison, "Visceral Influences on Brain and Behavior," in *Neuron* (2013) 77, 624–38; R. Dantzer, J. C. O'Connor, G. G. Freund, R. W. Johnson, and K. W. Kelley, "From Inflammation to Sickness and Depression: When the Immune System Subjugates the Brain," in *National Review of Neuroscience* (2008) 9: 46–56; N. A. Harrison, et al., "Neural Origins of Human Sickness in Interoceptive Responses to Inflammation," in *Biological Psychiatry* (2009) 66: 415–22 (2009); and M. P. Paulus and M. B. Stein, "Interoception in Anxiety and Depression," in *Brain Structure and Function* (2010) 214: 451–63.
15. Andrea Smith, *Conquest*, xvii.
16. Smith, xviii.
17. See Linda Curran, *101 Trauma-Informed Interventions*, 5–10.
18. Dominguez, 95–96.
19. The encomienda is a holding environment for a specific kind of panic, literally of a fear disguised as an intentional discovery and an intentional, baroque overcoding of the uncovered paradise promised in the dominant mythology. It was also an experiment. This intentionally designed system had an expected outcome but also a lot of unknowns, as a result of which violence was introduced as a manner of retaining control where uncertainty or improvisation might render the experiment impotent.
20. Hartman, *Scenes of Subjection*, 5.
21. I have been using the terms "survival" and "evolution," and I wish to stress how the emotional and affective responses to historical contexts like racialization, homophobia, and so on, contexts that these poets are responding to positively through lyric worldmaking, demonstrate simultaneously neuromodulation as well as culturally conditioned exhibitions of identity. A lot of research has expanded our understanding of how neuromodulators like dopamine, serotonin, and oxytocin interact with sociality and over a person's lifetime adapt to stimuli and overstimuli through plasticity; examples include, for instance, the work of Dr. Melenka, noted previously. Melenka's insights push the boundaries of neuroscience into humanistic implications and include new understanding of how empathy can be encouraged environmentally, and put another way, how belonging through ready-mades like white-body supremacy could be understood as having chemical as well educational sources.
22. Recent constitutional revolutions in Ecuador (2008), Bolivia (2009), and Chile (2022) have integrated Indigenous democratic practices as articles of government. I say "democratic," because these practices predate such an instrument of governance. In their contemporary context, however, these articles are meant to address centuries of antidemocratic, neoliberal violence and exploitation and move toward collective healing and progressive governance. It remains to be seen

how these articles will adapt to an overly capitalized world. But they are promising, nonetheless.
23. I'm using the notion of "recoding" here, as presented by Ramón Gutiérrez in *When Jesus Came, the Corn Mothers Went Away*. In that book, Gutiérrez historicizes how colonial Christianity recoded Indigenous and Native earth-centric symbology, effectively transforming earth-based practices into a fungible aesthetic, and then operationalizing that aesthetic to proliferate Christian mythos. Many critics of Gutiérrez note the intellectual erasure of the contemporary Indigenous experience through the demonstration of "coding" as a binary. As a poet, my interpretation is that our inherited landscapes provide opportunities for aesthetic plasticity. That does not mean certain politico-aesthetic moments have been clumsy in their borrowing or "unearthing" of Indigenous aesthetics. I cite Gutiérrez because the fundamental observation of aesthetic violence remains valuable for us to consider.
24. Dominguez, 86.
25. Bruce, *How to Go Mad Without Losing Your Mind*, 8.
26. Sharpe, *In the Wake*, 112.
27. Sharpe, 112. At no point in recent history has this "pseudoscience," as Sharpe identifies the logic, been more apparent than in the actions of Ron DeSantis as governor of Florida, who operationalizes our history of slavery to argue that Black bodies benefited from slavery, citing Clarence Thomas as an example.
28. Linklater, *Decolonizing Trauma Work*, 33.
29. Smith, 32–33.
30. Linklater, 32.
31. See Curran's *101 Trauma-Informed Interventions*.
32. Dominguez, 4.
33. March 6, 2019, Immigration and Border Security Secretary Nielsen denies "children are put in cages.... We don't use cages for children," she argued. When pressed on the issue, however, she conceded: "To my knowledge CPB never *purposefully* put a child in a cage."
34. Dominguez, 67.
35. Dominguez, 19.
36. Menakem, 59–61. The point is that, building on Joy DeGruy's work, *Post Traumatic Slave Syndrome*, on the 500-plus years of trauma endured during slavery, it stands to reason that an analysis of traumatic exposure is necessary for understanding white-body supremacy as a cultural container of chronic exposure.
37. Alexander, "Trayvon Generation."
38. The permissibility of white anger trumps equity at every opportunity. Cable, in 1903, noted how Emancipation gave white northerners and southerners an implicit bias on which to unite. We are living the aftermath of this collusion.
39. Dominguez, 86.
40. Dominguez, 14.

post/nation

1. Diné Yazhí, *Ancestral Memory*, 9.
2. For more on the geographic-experiential tension between transparent and multiscalar environments, see Katherine McKittrick's *Demonic Grounds*.
3. I arrive at this term, unpacked further in what follows, through the work of Ellie Hernández.
4. Albery Whitman, *The Rape of Florida*. Whitman's text was originally published in 1884 and later reprinted. A copy is available from the Fisk University Library Special Collections. This passage is from Canto II, XXXIV, 21.
5. Walter Mignolo argues that artists working within the context of decolonial thinking and study recover the knowledge and information of felt experiences of contact and subjection/subjugation. The aesthetics are created from the sentient/sensory project he calls *aesthesis*. Mignolo uses this term to elaborate on connotations of senses in aesthetics to include emotional dimensions, which promote ways for healing. See Mignolo, "Decolonial Options and Artistic/AestheSic Entanglements."
6. I am indebted to the thinking of Harney and Moten regarding fugitivity, as well as the ontological framing of terror in Calvin Warren's writing. See for instance, his *Ontological Terror*.
7. This sort of poetic construct puts Whitman's "breach," and indeed the territorial setting, in conversation with more contemporary works like Gloria Anzaldúa's decolonial rewriting of the Mexico–US border (1987), specifically the concept of "raja" and the "thin" barbed wire her poetic speaker in *Borderlands/La Frontera* "calls home."
8. Ellie D. Hernández, *Postnationalism in Chicana/o Literature and Culture*, 18.
9. See Lisa Lowe, "History Hesitant," in *Social Text*, 85–107. How persons throughout the world have survived, and indeed live out the spatiotemporal effects of this "power differential," is the premise of what Lowe terms an "intimacy," a concept that we can in turn use here to illustrate the Native Black relationship to the Black Seminole nation.
10. One need only read the section on slavery in the President's Advisory Commission 1776 report (2021), which explains away American slavery as a matter of historical necessity and hemispheric coincidence, denying it as the egregious historical fact of violence responsible for, among other forms of genocide, a continuum that structures and norms contemporary forms of anti-Blackness (10–12). The report, which was taken down by the Biden administration, can be found here: https://trumpwhitehouse.archives.gov/wp-content/uploads/2021/01/The-Presidents-Advisory-1776-Commission-Final-Report.pdf.
11. This is not meant to propose a Eurocentrism regarding voice, especially a Black and Native voice, but rather present Whitman's formal approaches to his awareness of the canonical archive. Form ensures the longevity and existence of his

work into the future, continuing to occupy a place in what as he understood as the canonical archive of poetry. As Whitman notes in the dedication, "I confess that living instances of real merit only will correct the world's judgment and force its respect. To this end I have laid out my life. Modest enough to be patient, I am not too tame to assert that I have some hope of ultimately reaching the ears of my countrymen" (3). Demonstrating genre or formal fluency would ensure that the work would be preserved as a vehicle for his poetic-political theory.

12. Whitman, 5.
13. Whitman, 7.
14. I think specifically here of how Whitman's poetics might offer insight into how to read contemporary Black poetry, from M. NourbeSe Philip's *Zong!* to Douglas Kearney's various "sound systems," or what I frame in the next section as "patching."
15. Whitman, Canto I, IX, 12.
16. Whitman, Canto I, XIII, 14.
17. Whitman, Canto I, XVII, 15.
18. Calvin Warren, *Ontological Terror*, 15.
19. Warren, 15.
20. Whitman, Canto I, XVII, 15.
21. In this context I am also reminded of Kamau Brathwaite's "nation language" and the idea of the experience of the speakers of a language who are responsible for revolutionary actions in poetry. Brathwaite's descriptive foundation behind this term engages with a "sound system," or what he calls "software," of the Caribbean through observations of calypso and oral traditions, an extended observation of tides and people. Coincidentally, Brathwaite also invested heavily on "sound" in terms of real sonic networks like radio, recording equipment, his computer, and cameras. See *History of the Voice*, 309–13.
22. The question here is not of ranking which is worse, settler-colonialism or anti-Blackness. They are the same "weather," so to speak, and citing Christina Sharpe. Moreover, during the nineteenth century the terminology of anti-Blackness often inflected how Native and Indigenous identity was constructed, with many Native men often referred to as "*******" in newspapers and legal documents, particularly in advertisements seeking the "capture" of runaway slaves. This reveals how criminality narratives are often used to underscore racialization by deprioritizing mentions of race to law and order, but in so doing effectively racialized the commons and how liberty is practiced through it.
23. Whitman, Canto I, XXVIII, 19.
24. Whitman, LXXIII, 51. The 1882 edition of the poem redacts specific mention of Zachary Taylor, America's twelfth president, in office during the second Seminole War, using instead asterisks, "******'s."
25. Whitman, LXXIV, 52.
26. Whitman XI, 31.

27. Whitman XI, 31.
28. *Newton Kansan*, May 24, 1888, 4.
29. Effigy strung up by the Ku Klux Klan, Miami, Florida (1940), L1986030_01, Stetson Kennedy Papers, L1979-37, Southern Labor Archives. Special Collections and Archives, Georgia State University, Atlanta.
30. Joan Blaeu, *Atlas Maior* (1665). I would also include as a sort of triptych here Winslow Homer's "Florida Jungle," which portrays an unpopulated, almost impenetrable scene of palmettos in soft hues. Homer's "vacation" paintings, moreover, played an indirect role in promoting tourism and its networks and the narratives of "wildness" that attracted many Northeasterners to the area.
31. *The Weekly Floridian*, July 4, 1882. *Chronicling America: Historic American Newspapers*. Library of Congress. chroniclingamerica.loc.gov.
32. Another interesting echo is then White House advisor Kevin Hassett's May 25, 2020, briefing in which he calls for reopening the economy during the height of the COVID-19 pandemic (a call referenced in this book's first chapter, "soma"). Hassett similarly appeals to the liberal democratic ontology, taking the economy as a living organism while simultaneously referring to working people as "human stock." The perverse relationship he creates in that ontology with life and death is historical: life and whiteness are conflated beyond corporeal limits, but those limits are de-amplified for Black futurity. The result is what many have since called the "Death Cult" behind many of Trump's anti-life appeals to the confluence of matters: protests regarding anti-Blackness, and a call for the health of a universal civic body (including Black beings and other bodies deemed "Black" by white-body supremacist morality).
33. Whitman, Canto II, LXXI, 51.
34. During debates, delegates from the "nucleus," central, pro-bank cotton growers, argued against another *ex post facto* law that the "loco focos," anti-bank delegates saw as a way out of faith bonds. In what seemed like an impasse, the nucleus appealed to the other delegates by arguing that making something, which had been legal—faith bonds, as contracts—illegal, was similar to abolitionists' arguments that slavery should hence forth be illegal. See Moussalli, "Florida's Frontier Constitution."
35. *New York Times*, August 1, 1865.
36. Kelsie, "Blackened Debate," 65.
37. "A Conversation with James Baldwin," from the series *Negro: An American Promise*, aired June 24, 1963. WGBH Educational Foundation, WGBH Boston, MA.
38. DinéYazhí, 13.
39. The term "necropolitics" was first used by the Cameroonian historian and philosopher Achille Mbembe to describe the institutionalized death and sublife of African peoples through global Euro-Anglo centrism. The term has since been borrowed by other communities, most recently by the trans and trans of color

communities to articulate the pervasive death cult expressed in civic society as some other morality—Christianity or democratism, for example.
40. DinéYazhí's own framing of the book.
41. cárdenas, "Dark Shimmers," 161.
42. Blas and cárdenas, "Imaginary Computational Systems."
43. DinéYazhí, 15–16.
44. DinéYazhí, artist book, *An Infected Sunset*.
45. DinéYazhí, *Ancestral Memory*, 9.
46. DinéYazhí, 24.
47. Whitman, 4.
48. DinéYazhí, 22.
49. Whitman, Canto II, IX, 12.
50. DinéYazhí, 13.

¡vecinos!

1. "Stakes Is High," from the album *Stakes Is High* (Tommy Boy Music, 1996).
2. Mather, in *On Religion and Reason: A Puritan discussion of man's reason—and the proper use of reason 1718–1775*, "A Man of Reason."
3. Kenneth Goldsmith's "remix" performance of Michael Brown's autopsy report in 2015 remains an active example of pornotroping and the failure of a poet in attempting a paradigm shift without shifting their own embodied positionality. Anger, as somatic, is not a "performance" in a diegetic or meta way.
4. Sharpe, 116.
5. cárdenas, "Dark Shimmers," 169.
6. See Kramer, Guillory, and Hancock, "Experimental Evidence of Massive-Scale Emotional Contagion through Social Networks."
7. Kearney, *Sho*, 46.
8. Ahmed, *Living a Feminist Life*, 34.
9. Kearney, *Sho*, 49. In Spanish, "vecino" means neighbor. In the parlance of Empire, a "vecino" was a landowning citizen (as opposed to a "residente"). "Vecino" meant "freeman."
10. Again, Kenneth Goldsmith.
11. Vicuña, *Precario/Precarious*.
12. Walter Mignolo calls this confluence of material and embodied realities the colonial matrices of modernity.
13. Morrow, *Marginalia*, 52.
14. Morrow, 51.
15. Kearney, *Sho*, 7.
16. Menakem, 18–20.
17. Following a rather deep dive, I can confirm commentor @KevinoftheCosmos's whiteness, and fragility.

18. White bodies when they exhibit white fragility are not particularly in a vulnerable state as I am thinking it, but rather a defensive/reflexive stance while in the presence of dark-skinned people. It's a grievance. The understanding of "properties" pertains to those descriptive fatalisms of a binary nature: fear/safety, criminal/hero, servant/master. Bodies of color have some feelings about these binary descriptions, which through repetition blend into definition. We get a little angry of always being wedged into the white subconscious through mundane public performances of social life.
19. Morrow, 81.
20. Morrow, 81.
21. Kearney, *Sho*, 9.
22. Gomez Moreno and Mignolo, *Estéticas decoloniales*, 15.

dreams

1. Erin Manning, *Always More Than One*, 9.
2. cárdenas, "Pregnancy" (poetry/media performance), in "Reproductive Futures in Trans of Color Feminism," *TSQ, yen* 56.
3. https://michacardenas.sites.ucsc.edu/pregnancy/.
4. cárdenas, "Pregnancy," 50.
5. Richerson and Boyd, *Not by Genes Alone*, 253.
6. Victor, 65.
7. Taylor, *The Archive and the Repertoire*, xvii.
8. cárdenas, "Pregnancy," 51.
9. Foster, *Genre and White Supremacy*, 16.
10. Foster, 16.
11. Victor, 65.
12. Victor, 53.
13. Victor, 53.
14. Victor, 57–58.
15. Claudia Rankine, *Plot*, 23.
16. The historical study at the center of the epigenetics story is the Överkalix study, first published in 2002. See Kaati, Bygren, and Edvinsson, "Cardiovascular and Diabetes Mortality Determined by Nutrition During Parents' and Grandparents' Slow Growth Period. *European Journal of Human Genetics* (2002) 10: 682–88. https://doi.org/10.1038/sj.ejhg.5200859.
17. Kearney, *Optic Subwoof*.
18. See Mouffe, *The Democratic Paradox*, 14.
19. Barrett, *How Emotions Are Made*, 30.
20. Rankine, *Just Us*, 25.

bibliography

Adler-Bolton, Beatrice, and Artie Vierkant. *Health Communism*. Brooklyn, NY: Verso, 2022.
Ahmed, Sara. *The Cultural Politics of Emotion*. New York: Routledge Taylor & Francis, 2004.
Ahmed, Sara. *Living a Feminist Life*. Durham, NC: Duke University Press, 2017.
Alexander, Elizabeth. *Body of Life*. San Fernando, CA: Tia Chucha, 1996.
Alexander, Elizabeth. "The Trayvon Generation." *New Yorker*. June 15, 2020. https://www.newyorker.com/magazine/2020/06/22/the-trayvon-generation.
Barrett, Lisa Feldman. *How Emotions Are Made*. London: Pan Books, 2017.
Bitzer, Lloyd. "The Rhetorical Situation." *Philosophy & Rhetoric* (1992) 25 (1): 1–14.
Blas, Zach, and micha cárdenas. "Imaginary Computational Systems: Queer Technologies and Transreal Aesthetics." *AI and Society* (2013) 28 (Fall). https://doi.org/10.1007/s00146-013-0502-y.
Brathwaite, Kamau. *History of the Voice*. London: New Beacon Books, 1984.
Bruce, La Marr Jurelle. *How to Go Mad without Losing Your Mind: Madness and Black Radical Creativity*. Durham, NC: Duke University Press, 2020.
Cable, George Washington, and University of North Carolina at Chapel Hill University Library. *The Negro Question*. New York: Scribner's, 1903. Internet Archive. https://archive.org/details/negroquestiooocabl/page/n5/mode/2up.
cárdenas, micha. "Dark Shimmers: The Rhythm of Necropolitical Affect in Digital Media." *Trap Door: Trans Cultural Production and the Politics of Visibility* (2017): 161–81.
cárdenas, micha. "Pregnancy." *TSQ: Transgender Studies Quarterly* (2016) 3 (1–2): 48–57. https://doi.org/10.1215/23289252-3334187.
Chan, Dorothy. *Revenge of the Asian Woman*. Doha, Qatar: Diode Editions, 2019.
Culler, Jonathan. "Lyric, History, and Genre." *New Literary History* (2009) 40 (4): 879–99. https://doi.org/10.1353/nlh.0.0121.
Curran, Linda A. *101 Trauma-Informed Interventions: Activities, Exercises and Assignments to Move the Client and Therapy Forward*. Eau Claire, WI: Pesi Publishing et Media, 2013.
DinéYazhí, Demian. *Ancestral Memory*. Portland: Pur Dubois Press, 2016.
Dominguez, Angel. *Desgraciado*. Brooklyn, NY: Nightboat Books, 2022.

Foster, Travis M. *Genre and White Supremacy in the Postemancipation United States*. Oxford, U.K.: Oxford University Press, 2019.

Gómez Moreno, Pedro Pablo, and Walter Mignolo. *Estéticas decoloniales [recurso electronico]*. Bogotá: Sección de Publicaciones Universidad Distrital Fancisco José de Caldas, 2012.

Gutiérrez, Ramón A. *When Jesus Came, the Corn Mothers Went Away: Marriage, Sexuality, and Power in New Mexico, 1500–1846*. Stanford, CA: Stanford University Press, 2006.

Harney, Stefano, and Fred Moten. *The Undercommons: Fugitive Planning and Black Study*. Wivenhoe, U.K.: Minor Compositions, 2013.

Hartman, Saidiya V. *Scenes of Subjection: Terror, Slavery, and Self-Making in Nineteenth-Century America*. New York and Oxford, U.K.: Oxford University Press, 1997.

Hernández, Ellie D. *Postnationalism in Chicana/O Literature and Culture*. Austin, TX: University of Texas Press, 2010.

Hicok, Bob. "The Promise of American Poetry—Utne." *Utne Reader* (July 9, 2019). https://www.utne.com/arts/new-american-poetry-zm0z19uzhoe/?fbclid=IwAR1vp4vnYhP1DByS8xuxHGP8DNaMqryxMwoo8WQ1NGlwB16PvGu666iF9Gc.

Jadhav, Adam. "Was It Rural Populism? Returning to the Country, 'Catching Up,' and Trying to Understand the Trump Vote." *Journal of Rural Studies* (October 2020): 553–69. https://doi.org/10.1016/j.jrurstud.2020.10.008.

Kearney, Douglas. *Optic Subwoof*. Seattle, WA: Wave Books, 2022.

Kearney, Douglas. *Sho*. Seattle, WA: Wave Books, 2022.

Kelsie, Amber E. "Blackened Debate at the End of the World." *Philosophy & Rhetoric* (2019) 52 (1): 63–70. https://doi.org/10.5325/philrhet.52.1.0063.

Kramer, A. D., J. E. Guillory, and J. T. Hancock. "Experimental Evidence of Massive-Scale Emotional Contagion through Social Networks." *Proceedings of the National Academy of Sciences of the United States of America* (2014) 111 (24): 8788–90. https://doi.org/10.1073/pnas.1320040111.

Lezra, Jacques. *Defective Institutions*. New York, NY: Fordham University Press, 2024.

Linklater, Renee. *Decolonizing Trauma Work: Indigenous Stories and Strategies*. Halifax: Fernwood, 2014.

Lowe, Lisa. "History Hesitant." *Social Text* (2015) 33 (4 (125)): 85–107. https://doi.org/10.1215/01642472-3315790.

Manning, Erin. *Always More Than One: Individuation's Dance*. Durham, NC: Duke University Press, 2013.

Martín-Baró, Ignacio. "Political Violence and War as Causes of Psychological Trauma in El Salvador." *International Journal of Mental Health* (1989)18 (1): 3–20.

Martín-Baró, Ignacio. *Writings for a Liberation Psychology*. Translated by Adrianne Aron and Shawn Corne. London, U.K., and Cambridge, MA: Harvard University Press, 1994.

Mather, Cotton. 1718. "On Religion and Reason." Accessed July 10, 2024. https://nationalhumanitiescenter.org/pds/becomingamer/ideas/text1/religionreason.pdf.

McKittrick, Katherine. *Demonic Grounds: Black Women and the Cartographies of Struggle*. Minneapolis: University of Minnesota Press, 2013.

Menakem, Resmaa. *My Grandmother's Hands: Healing Racial Trauma in Our Minds and Bodies*. London and Scoresby, U.K.: Penguin Books, Penguin Random House, 2021.

Mignolo, Walter. "Decolonial Options and Artistic/AestheSic Entanglements: An Interview with Walter Mignolo." By Rubén Gaztambide-Fernández. *Decolonization: Indigeneity, Education and Society* (2014) 3 (1): 196–212. https://jps.library.utoronto.ca/index.php/des/article/view/21310/17389.

Morrow, Juno. *Marginalia*. Clash Books, 2020.

Moten, Fred. *Stolen Life*. Durham, NC: Duke University Press, 2018.

Mouffe, Chantal. *The Democratic Paradox*. London: Verso, 2000.

Moussalli, Stephanie D. "Florida's Frontier Constitution: The Statehood, Banking and Slavery Controversies." *Florida Historical Quarterly* (2000) 74 (4): 423–39. https://www.jstor.org/stable/30148879.

Muñoz, José Esteban. *The Sense of Brown*. Edited by Tavia Amolo Ochieng' Nyongó and Joshua Takano Chambers-Letson. Durham, NC: Duke University Press, 2020.

"The Negro and the American Promise." Indiana University, Bloomington, Audio-Visual Center, Media Collections Online, 1962. https://media.dlib.indiana.edu/media_objects/hh63sw148#:~:text=Brings%20together%20four%20prominent%20Negro.

Newman, Mark. "Election Maps." Department of Physics and Center for the Study of Complex Systems, University of Michigan, 2016. https://websites.umich.edu/~mejn/election/2016/.

Nguyen, Joshua. *Come Clean*. Madison, WI: University of Wisconsin Press, 2021.

Nguyen, Joshua. "Q&A with Joshua Nguyen, Author of *Come Clean*." Interview with Gauri Awasthi. *Offing*. September 16, 2022. https://theoffingmag.com/interviews/qa-with-joshua-nguyen-author-of-come-clean/.

Rankine, Claudia. *Just Us: An American Conversation*. Minneapolis, MN: Graywolf Press, 2020.

Rankine, Claudia. *Plot*. New York, NY: Grove Press, 2001.

Rawls, John. *A Theory of Justice*. Cambridge, MA: Harvard University Press, 1971.

Richerson, Peter J., and Robert Boyd. *Not by Genes Alone: How Culture Transformed Human Evolution*. Chicago, IL: University of Chicago Press, 2005.

Said, Edward W. *Beginnings: Intentions and Method*. New York, NY: Basic Books, 1975.

Scully, Matthew. *Democratic Anarchy*. New York, NY: Fordham University Press, 2024.

Sharpe, Christina. *In the Wake: On Blackness and Being*. Durham, NC: Duke University Press, 2016.

Smith, Andrea. *Conquest: Sexual Violence and American Indian Genocide*. Durham, NC: Duke University Press, 2015.

Taylor, Diana. *The Archive and the Repertoire: Performing Cultural Memory in the Americas*. Durham, NC: Duke University Press, 2003.

Victor, Divya. *Curb*. Brooklyn, NY: Nightboat Books, 2021.

Vicuña, Cecilia. *Precario/Precarious*. New York: Tanam Press, 1983.

Walsh, Jessica J., Daniel J. Christoffel, and Robert C. Malenka. "Neural Circuits Regulating Prosocial Behaviors." *Neuropsychopharmacology* (2023) 48 (1): 79–89. https://doi.org/10.1038/s41386-022-01348-8.

Warren, Calvin L. *Ontological Terror: Blackness, Nihilism, and Emancipation*. Durham, NC, and London: Duke University Press, 2018.

Wells, Ida B. "Southern Horrors: Lynch Law in All Its Phases by Ida B. Wells." 1892. Charlottesville, VA: Encyclopedia Virginia. https://encyclopediavirginia.org/primary-documents/southern-horrors-lynch-law-in-all-its-phases-by-ida-b-wells-1892/.

White, Michael. *Maps of Narrative Practice*. New York: Norton, 2007.

Whitman, Albery Allson. *The Rape of Florida*. Miami, FL: Mnemosyne Publishing, 1884. https://books.google.com/books?id=wOxJAAAAMAAJ&printsec=frontcover&source=gbs_ge_summary_r&cad=0#v=onepage&q&f=false.

Wynter, Sylvia. "Unsettling the Coloniality of Being/Power/Truth/Freedom: Towards the Human, after Man, Its Overrepresentation—an Argument." *CR: New Centennial Review* (2003) 3 (3): 257–337.

The New American Canon

purplish: poetry anger publics
by José Felipe Alvergue

Half a Million Strong:
Crowds and Power from
Woodstock to Coachella
by Gina Arnold

Violet America:
Regional Cosmopolitanism in
U.S. Fiction since the Great Depression
by Jason Arthur

The Meanings of J. Robert Oppenheimer
by Lindsey Michael Banco

Neocolonial Fictions of the
Global Cold War
edited by Steven Belletto and Joseph Keith

Workshops of Empire:
Stegner, Engle, and American Creative
Writing during the Cold War
by Eric Bennett

Novel Competition:
American Fiction and the
Cultural Economy, 1965–1999
by Evan Brier

Places in the Making:
A Cultural Geography of
American Poetry
by Jim Cocola

The Legacy of David Foster Wallace
edited by Samuel Cohen and
Lee Konstantinou

Writing Wars:
Authorship and American War Fiction,
WWI to Present
by David F. Eisler

Race Sounds:
The Art of Listening in
African American Literature
by Nicole Brittingham Furlonge

Postmodern/Postwar—and After:
Rethinking American Literature
edited by Jason Gladstone,
Andrew Hoberek, and Daniel Worden

After the Program Era:
The Past, Present, and Future of
Creative Writing in the University
edited by Loren Glass

Hope Isn't Stupid:
Utopian Affects in Contemporary
American Literature
by Sean Austin Grattan

It's Just the Normal Noises:
Marcus, Guralnick, No Depression,
and the Mystery of Americana Music
by Timothy Gray

Wrong:
A Critical Biography of Dennis Cooper
by Diarmuid Hester

Reverse Colonization:
Science Fiction, Imperial Fantasy,
and Alt-victimhood
by David M. Higgins

Profiles and Plotlines:
Data Surveillance in Twenty-first
Century Literature
by Katherine D. Johnston

Art Essays:
A Collection
edited by Alexandra Kingston-Reese

Contemporary Novelists and the Aesthetics
of Twenty-First Century American Life
by Alexandra Kingston-Reese

American Unexceptionalism:
The Everyman and the Suburban
Novel after 9/11
by Kathy Knapp

Visible Dissent:
Latin American Writers, Small U.S.
Presses, and Progressive Social Change
by Teresa V. Longo

Pynchon's California
edited by Scott McClintock and
John Miller

Richard Ford and the Ends of Realism
by Ian McGuire

Novel Subjects:
Authorship as Radical Self-Care in
Multiethnic American Narratives
by Leah A. Milne

William Gibson and the Futures of
Contemporary Culture
edited by Mitch R. Murray and
Mathias Nilges

Poems of the American Empire:
The Lyric Form in the Long
Twentieth Century
by Jen Hedler Phillis

Reading Capitalist Realism
edited by Alison Shonkwiler and
Leigh Claire La Berge

The Global Frontier:
Postwar Travel in American Literature
by Eric Strand

Technomodern Poetics:
The American Literary Avant-Garde at
the Start of the Information Age
by Todd F. Tietchen

Contested Terrain:
Suburban Fiction and
U.S. Regionalism, 1945–2020
by Keith Wilhite

Ecospatiality:
A Place-Based Approach to
American Literature
by Lowell Wyse

How to Revise a True War Story:
Tim O'Brien's Process of Textual
Production
by John K. Young